INSPIRATIONAL STORIES OF WOMEN
LEADING, THRIVING, AND BREAKING BARRIERS

LATINAS RISING UP IN HR VOL. II

PRISCILLA GUASSO

LATINAS RISING UP IN HR ®

© Copyright 2022, Latinas Rising Up In HR.
All rights reserved.

All rights reserved. No portion of this book may be reproduced by mechanical, photographic or electronic process, nor may it be stored in a retrieval system, transmitted in any form or otherwise be copied for public use or private use without written permission of the copyright owner.

This book is a compilation of stories from numerous people who have each contributed a chapter and is designed to provide inspiration to our readers.

It is sold with the understanding that the publisher and the individual authors are not engaged in the rendering of psychological, legal, accounting or other professional advice. The content and views in each chapter are the sole expression and opinion of its author and not necessarily the views of Fig Factor Media, LLC.

For more information visit:
Latinas Rising Up In HR | www.latinasrisingupinhr.com
Fig Factor Media, LLC | www.figfactormedia.com

Cover Design & Layout by Juan Manuel Serna Rosales
Logo Design by AntiH: Miguel Aranda & Alonso Hernandez Jimenez

Printed in the United States of America

ISBN: 978-1-957058-14-6
Library of Congress Control Number: 2022916995

Regardless of what community you are from, you have copies of keys to open doors for others, and we invite you to be an active part of our journey. I dedicate this book to you. Believe in the change that you can create and act on it.

Table of Contents:

Acknowledgments 6
Preface by Catherine Ibarra-O'Connell 10
Introduction by Priscilla Guasso 16

Author Chapters 22
   PRISCILLA GUASSO 23
     What Battles Are You Going Through?
   JOSELIN ZENEIDA SANZ 33
     Trust Your Values Will Guide You
   ANGÉLICA HERRERA-LÓPEZ 41
     Breaking Through Limited Beliefs
   ARLENE NAIRN 51
     Yo Soy. I am.
   VANESSA DURÁN 61
     Poniéndome Las Pilas
   BRENDA SÁNCHEZ-PINEDA 71
     Strength & Perseverance – It's in Our Blood
   ARIANA J. PAZ 81
     Riding the Waves of Constant Change
   KAYLA CASTRO KRUGER 91
     ¡Sí Se Puede!
   STEFANIE FURNISS 99
     Every Day the Clock Resets

MONICA CRISTAL GAONA 111
It's Never Too Late To Achieve Your Dreams

ANGÉLICA PATLÁN 121
Breaking Into HR, The Nontraditional Way

ARELY LAGUNAS 131
Failing Forward: Leaning into Our Strengths & Growth

CAROLINA M. VEIRA 143
Am I the Only One in the Room or Am I Dreaming?

YARED S. OLIVEROS 153
Un Día A La Vez

ARLENE RODRÍGUEZ 163
Building Resilience Through Life's Seasons

Resources 173
About the Author 176

Acknowledgments

With this volume, I would like to thank my husband, **Jorge Guasso,** for his tireless support in lifting me up when I ran into so many struggles. He saw the true sweat and tears that went into all that's been built and never ceases to encourage me to push through and rise up. Come what may, it's our Golden Hour <3

To **my family,** this past year it was definitely a family project! I love each of you so much for the encouraging texts in family chats, 1:1 calls, or through my love language of gifts. Thank you for giving my wings wind to keep flying higher.

A big shoutout to my sister-in-law, **Jessica Guasso**, for joining my team and helping me execute on deadlines, creative, social media, and event planning. You have such a creative eye and imagination. I cannot wait to see the amazing work you continue to do in the future as you follow your curiosity! Keep dreaming big…you will achieve it!

I am extremely grateful to Fig Factor Media (FFM) for helping us bring Volume 2 to life and expanding our dreams into another anthology. I will forever be grateful to you **Jackie Camacho Ruiz, Gaby Hernández Franch, Kylie Knur**, and the rest of the FFM dream team for continuing to elevate our impact to another level.

A special thank you to my sister-in-crime, **Jessica Galván**, who worked side by side with our publisher and authors to help bring the stories of our authors to life. This is one of the hardest jobs because it requires listening to the authors while drawing out their feelings and helping them put it into writing. Thank you for your tireless effort behind not just editing Volume 2, but for caring deeply that each author loved their story.

To our **newly published authors of Volume 2:** CONGRATULATIONS!!! You are each such a bright light to me and the reason why I believe in what we do. You have all shown me that behind each amazing smile is a true guerrera (warrior). All of your successes prove that the sky's the limit and together we can achieve anything! Thank you for trusting me in this process and saying "yes" to not only investing in yourself, but for truly believing that your story can open doors for future HR leaders. Your continued mentorship and sponsorship to Latinas Rising Up In HR will make the change.

Book Sisters of Volume 1...wow, words cannot describe the gratitude I have for all of you. Not just for what we've accomplished in the last two years, but because of the way you each showed up to welcome and encourage our Volume 2 authors. The actions I see behind our sisterhood demonstrate how deep our values run. You all are the definition of what it looks like to surround yourself with who you aspire to be while rising together. I am a better leader and person because of each of you.

Congratulations to our 2022 Leadership Award Winner and V1 author **Janine Ting Jansen** for supporting me and our authors in more ways than one this past year. You are an incredible leader and friend, Janine…"thank you" is not enough, and I hope you felt the love at our summit :)

Thank you to our 2021 Leadership Award winner and V1 author **Myriam Del Angel** for being my right-hand woman for our inaugural Leadership Summit & Book Launch as well as future projects. I cannot wait to see you continue to fly to new heights.

My heartfelt thanks to V1 author **Irma Reyes** and all our V1 authors for spearheading our first ever Latinas Rising Up In HR scholarship in 2021! You and all our authors are blessings in my life, loving me not just for what I do, but more importantly for who I am (flaws and all!). I hope you're all ready to one day be my madrinas!

Sara Lebens, my beautiful friend, thank you for reaching out to me that day almost two years ago and continuing to be a close mentor, sponsor, coach, and friend. You came in when I was at my most vulnerable and helped bring clarity, direction, vision, insights, support, and strength. I don't think you realize the impact you made on me…you truly are someone everyone needs in their corner. I am blessed to have you in my life.

To the leaders at University of Miami, CDW, Hyatt, Netflix, CareMax, Robertet, Topo Chico, and Fig Factor Media, I understand there are many organizations you can choose to partner with, and you chose to invest in us. I thank each of you for seeing the potential and value of the work we are implementing with our events, workshops, leadership summit, book launch, and scholarships. We need more organizations like yours that choose action over intention. With your continued support, I look forward to seeing our impact spread across the globe.

To the many leaders, friends, and HR professionals I've had the pleasure of working with or connected with on LinkedIn and have answered this calling of leadership with us: Thank you for your patience as we focused on our foundation, values, and future. The time is now, and I cannot wait to meet you in person and online as we look to launch our city activations in 2023! **Connect with us at www.LatinasRisingUpInHR.com and become a member today!**

PREFACE
By Catherine Ibarra-O'Connell
Regional VP, Human Resources – Latin America & Caribbean

A few years ago, Priscilla Guasso told me she was going to produce an anthology of stories called *Latinas Rising Up in HR*. I was in awe of her for conceiving a way for Latinas in HR to tell their important stories, and my heart swelled with amazement and pride at what she ultimately achieved. Anybody who has ever written a book will tell you that writing a book is a lot like giving birth. So with that metaphor, asking me to write the preface makes me feel very much like a godmother to one of her children—a role I am happy and honored to accept.

At this point, Priscilla has not just launched a book series—she has launched a movement. I wasn't surprised at the success of *Latinas Rising Up in HR*. Priscilla has always had a knack for connecting with people; it's one of the reasons I hired her to be my "number two" while working together at Hyatt Hotels Corporation. I had just been named regional vice president of human resources in Latin America and the Caribbean. I loved the fact that she applied not from HR, but from DEI. She not only could bring people together but was dedicated to helping them break through barriers to success. Together we embarked upon a great adventure in a new territory.

THE ROAD TO VP

In 2012, I was the HR Director for the Hyatt Orlando Airport when I saw the Hyatt posting for the VP position. The company's goals were ambitious. They wanted to grow from eight hotels in the territory to thirty within a five-year period. What a challenge!

I've heard it said that men apply for jobs if they meet 80 percent of the application requirements, but women don't do so unless they meet 100 percent of them. This was perhaps the first time I applied for a position knowing that I did not meet 100 percent of the requirements. However, I was convinced I could do the job, and would quickly learn what I needed to know. So, despite the other senior and more experienced people that were sure to apply, I threw my hat in the ring.

When I passed the first round and was called in to interview, I realized I had to seriously consider what might differentiate me for this role and sell it well in the interview. I decided it wasn't that I was a woman, or a Latina, or even that I spoke Spanish—it was that I truly was bicultural.

My parents were from Ecuador, but they moved to New York City as a young couple. My father worked for the United Nations and I ended up living in various South American countries throughout my childhood. I can credit my success in business to my father. He encouraged my sisters and me to leave home and pursue a career. He told us we could marry, but we should remain independent and have a career so we would never have to depend on our husband.

I attended Florida International University for hospitality management in Miami, and there I started my career in Hyatt as an intern at the front desk. I found Hyatt to have an excellent culture for women, and especially women who aspire to a leadership role. I didn't feel any roadblocks to succeeding there as a Latina. In fact, for a bilingual woman working in Miami, there were even more doors to be opened.

As women, it's our responsibility to elevate, not undermine each other. I'm sorry to say that working with my first Latina boss was not a pleasant experience. She was competitive, and in my opinion, she tried to cut my wings whenever I wanted to fly. I worried that the way she managed people would damage the reputation of Latina managers at the company. I wanted to be the supportive manager she wasn't, and luckily, I had people up the chain of command, of all races and nationalities, who believed I would. They advocated for my promotions and helped me reach new heights.

One of my colleagues in hospitality told me she was given the career advice to minimize her "Latina-ness." She took classes to lose her accent and did her best to look and sound as "American" as possible. That may have worked for her, but I took the opposite approach. I embrace who I am and share it joyfully. I use Spanish words with humor and jokingly mispronounce American words. It makes me a relatable and memorable colleague and allows me to stay true to myself. I planned to do the same as I pursued my new career as VP.

However, before I walked into the interview room, I had prepared well, with mock interviews from colleagues and with the toughest interviewer of all—my husband. He thought I would be great for the position and always encouraged me to follow my dreams. Just as there's a great woman behind every man, there's a great man behind any woman trying to move up the ladder.

The day finally arrived, and I walked into the room and sat down facing a panel of three male executives from corporate upper management. I made them see my bicultural advantage, and how my experience and ability to work with people throughout Latin America was my special sauce. I understood the certain customs and protocols in each region that help people connect appropriately with others. They believed in me, and I was offered the job soon after. The first few years were not easy, there was so much to learn, and to this day I continue learning. Fortunately, back then I had a great partner to take on the challenge: Priscilla Guasso!

WOMEN HELPING WOMEN

I've always felt a great responsibility to mentor other women whenever possible. Women are so often underestimated for our multitasking abilities, resourcefulness, and ambition to rise. In my new VP position, I see this often and do my best to make sure promotable women are valued and receive the promotions they deserve. For example, on one occasion I suggested promoting one of our female, high-level managers in South America to the top leadership role at one of our hotels. There was hesitancy on the part of the decision makers because she had just had a baby. Although maternity leave was ending, they thought she would feel too busy and overwhelmed to be starting a more challenging position, in a different country no less. I told them it was for her to decide and fought for her to get the offer. It was a proud moment for me when she excitedly accepted. She also told me how valued and appreciated by the company she felt for giving the offer when we did.

Another time we had just promoted a wonderfully talented female general manager in one of our countries, when she requested to use the company's educational benefits to pursue a master's degree. At the time, she had just moved to a new country, gotten married, adopted a son, in addition to a new and demanding job. Again, her boss was hesitant to approve, as he worried she could not do it all. I advocated for her, and her studies were approved. Not only did she do an amazing job in her new role, but she was awarded Business Person of the Year by the home city of her hotel.

Stories like these illustrate a basic theme of the first volume of this series. The inaugural book was like a rally cry that we exist. This second volume shows that Latinas are a force to be reckoned with in the field of HR. The stories within are all different, but many are about finding the right balance between professional and personal fulfillment. Latinas are prone to explain their accomplishments as luck, but actually, they achieve everything through their own hard work and vision.

This volume of *Latinas Rising Up in HR* is part of an evolution of a close sisterhood. We need to help each other succeed. We must be dedicated to climbing the ladder, then reaching back down to pull up the ones coming behind.

I'm proud to say that Hyatt's goals for DEI include doubling the amount of female vice presidents in the company by 2025. As with most industries, the pandemic set us back, but has also helped our culture create a more flexible work environment in terms of time, place, and technology. There's a place for confident, upwardly mobile Latinas in HR at Hyatt, and definitely in our society at large. The time is right. We are here, we can do more, and we're open to the challenge!

Catherine Ibarra-O'Connell
Regional VP, Human Resources
Latin America & Caribbean
Hyatt

Introduction

It's been two years since I started leading an idea that constantly left me with more questions than answers. Throughout this whole journey of building Latinas Rising Up In HR, I kept asking myself, how am I going to make this happen? As I reflect on the highs and lows of these past two years, the words of countless influential leaders come to mind: "Nothing is done alone." This couldn't be further from the truth. If this is your first touchpoint with Latinas Rising Up In HR, welcome to what is both an inspiring book and one of the most authentic communities intentionally built to connect Latinas and Allies in HR. We welcome you to join us in doing exactly what our title says...elevating the voices of Latinas Rising Up In HR.

For everyone that supported our first book, thank you for answering the leadership call to further sponsor and amplify our voice. We gathered virtually to show that if we are all behind a purpose, strengthened by values and action...change is possible. What started as a movement right before the pandemic in 2020 now offers six scholarships to graduate and undergraduate students as well as countless opportunities for our authors to speak, grow, promote, and inspire change across all countries. In these two years, I am humbled and honored at seeing how we've grown a following of over two thousand women and allies across the globe. We have witnessed how one inspirational story can have a powerful ripple effect in reminding us that we are not alone and that it is our responsibility as leaders in HR to lift up the next generation.

ONE STORY CAN MAKE ALL THE DIFFERENCE

In order to advocate for change, it's important for us to know the statistics of where our biggest strengths and gaps are for our community. In my years of being around amazing leaders, one thing I encourage us all to remember is "what gets measured gets done." We are lifted up by amazing organizations like HACE, NHCC, HACR, Hispanic Star, and LCDA among many others that are leading the charge with measuring what is happening within our community, and I invite you to support them as they do us.

When I am asked, "Priscilla, why are you doing another book?" my response will always be because we each have a responsibility to use our voice and influence real change in our circle of influence…and for us that means from within HR to close the gaps. Why do the gaps continue to grow when we see more Latinas graduating from college and graduate schools? After the pandemic, Latinas continue to be impacted by wage gaps, are more likely to leave the corporate environment due to a lack of representation at senior leader roles, need greater access to sponsors and have less opportunities for board seats. If you're not already aware, this is why Latinas Rising Up In HR matters...

- *1% of board seats are Latina[1]*
- *2 Latina CEOs exist within the Fortune 500[2]*
- *1.6% of executives are Latinas[3]*
  - *Of 92 companies in the S&P 100 reviewed by USA TODAY, 18 had no Latinas in senior executive positions.[4]*
- *3% of senior level positions are Latinas[5]*
- *4.4% of managers are Latinas with 3.2% of professionals as Latinas[6]*
  - *Only 5% of Latino professionals in large companies have a sponsor, research shows.[7]*
  - *For every 100 men promoted to manager, only 71 Latinas are promoted.[8]*
  - *76% of Latinos repress parts of who they are at work[9]*

[1-2] "2021 LATINO BOARD MONITOR," 2021, https://www.latinocorporatedirectors.org/docs/LCDA_2021_Latino_Board_Monitor.pdf.
[3-4,6] "Only Two Latinas Have Been CEO of a Fortune 500 Company. Why so Few Hispanic Women Make It to the Top." USA Today. Gannett Satellite Information Network, August 2, 2022. https://www.usatoday.com/story/money/2022/08/02/hispanic-latina-business-demographics-executive/10157271002/.
[5,8,10-11] "HISPANIC HERITAGE MONTH 2022 BRIEFING BOOK" (Hispanic Star, 2022), https://hispanicstar.org/wp-content/uploads/2022/04/HHM-2022-BriefingBook.pdf.
[7,9] "U.S. Latinos Feel They Can't Be Themselves at Work," Harvard Business Review, October 11, 2016, https://hbr.org/2016/10/u-s-latinos-feel-they-cant-be-themselves-at-work.

- *Latinas are the lowest paid segment in the US, making only 0.57 cents for every dollar made by white, non-Hispanic men.*[10]
- *During COVID-19, 21% of Latinas lost their jobs and 62% increased their family responsibilities during the pandemic.*[11]

For my visual learners, like me, various research shows that Latinas hold:

After you take a moment to truly take in the statistics above from all the work our community and allies have done, my question to you is, **how are you helping bridge the gap?** My vision with building a second volume is that it's one way to reach people inside and outside of our community to learn about different experiences we have not just as HR professionals, but as leaders in our homes and within our communities. These stories share experiences of how one person helped someone move forward, how a scholarship opened a door, or as simple as how a manager doing their job as a leader created development opportunities for a colleague. These stories are **the difference**. My focus is on the HR community because we are not exempt from going through similar obstacles of what our employees go through. Sometimes it's even harder for us to find the support to change an organization and alter the stats above. However, the difference is, as we each continue to elevate into levels of leadership, **it's imperative we honor how we got to where we are and advocate changes in the workplace to make opportunity not just equal, but more importantly: <u>equitable.</u>**

The biggest question companies are asking is, how do we bridge the gap for Latinas? I go back to what I stated above: what gets measured is what gets done. **It's finding the inequities, pulling together financial support, and leveraging your leadership to influence actionable change. As a new generation emerges into our workforce year over year, the time is now.**

In the following chapters, you will read heartfelt, raw, honest experiences of tough upbringings, traumas, uncertainty, and disappointments. I encourage you to read them with an open mind, as stories from the past, but with a lesson to be learned. Each author has vulnerably opened up to share different parts of their personal experiences with microaggressions, traumas, impostor syndrome, battling inner critics, or just fighting the statistics above to achieve their dreams as current or past HR professionals. That being said, their career is just one layer of who they proudly are, and what many times goes unseen is what we've persevered through to shine so bright today. I invite you to walk into **just a moment** of our lives in this book and find two minutes to encourage our authors with a review on Amazon with what you learned. It takes great strength and leadership to open up a part of your story to the world that perhaps hasn't been previously shared. As we continue to reach for our dreams, know that success for us is not defined by our profession. Success with this book is defined by having the opportunity to connect 1:1 with you in your own journey to feel seen, heard, and valued. If we can continue to be honest with what we've experienced and come together as Latinas and allies in HR, I know one thing will happen for sure: **there is no limit to the actionable impact we can achieve in our circle of influence.**

Author Chapters

WHAT BATTLES ARE YOU GOING THROUGH?

PRISCILLA GUASSO

"Take small steps first, celebrate your wins and the "how" will eventually come into place."

WALKING TOWARDS THE UNKNOWN

As I've ventured into this space of becoming a leadership catalyst and lean ahead to inspire change through action, I personally battle with **believing in the power of one**. Yes, you heard me right. Everyone has something they are constantly working on. Now, if they're ready to openly share their struggle, that's a different story. Since I was a young girl, I have continued to battle a thing that we now call "your inner critic." At one point in my life I thought, *oh my goodness, am I a person that sees the world as a cup half empty?!* The answer is no, my life is focused on choosing to find the positive…but if you were in my mind…my inner doubts can put my dreams on halt by looping criticisms such as "Is this your best? What makes you think you can do this? Why do you think it can be done? How will you do it? How? How? How?" I've been around some of the most amazing organizations and leaders that have encouraged me to be the best, produce the best, and to be proud of the planning process just as much as the end product. I will tell you what I continue to tell myself: **the power of one is where we start. Then multiply it.** It is through amazing leaders like Catherine O'Connell in our preface that took me under her wing to grow our careers in Latin America & the Caribbean, Nikki Massey who listened to my dream on a Saturday morning and believed in me, Kristy Seidel who invested in me with constant affirmations when I needed it most, Katherine Armstrong who has always been just a phone call away readily available to lift me up and Sara Lebens who took a leap to coach me when I least knew I would need it. They among many others leaders remind me of the power of one…and that it's not just an idea, but a decision and a way of life. As you continue to follow me on this journey, my hope is that as I choose to grow in this belief myself, you will too and that #TogetherWeRise.

I believe that at some point in our journey society has ingrained in us that if we do not know our purpose, our path, or our end game…we are LOST. **But truly, are we?**

After focusing intently on my personal and professional development these past years, coupled with coaching leaders across all levels, let me bring you into a secret: **NO ONE HAS IT FIGURED OUT.** Some of the most successful adults achieved the epitome of their careers or life goals through following their curiosity, which ultimately led them to their passion and purpose. We crave answers, focus, direction, and look in so many places for it. The truth is you have it within and it intersects between your heart, head, and instinct. But the decisions we make in life either lead us closer or further away from finding it.

In the last two years, it wasn't the pandemic that worried me or caused me angst. It has always been a foundational fear of the unknown. The same lives in my day to day. My therapist and recent coach challenged me to spend more time thinking about what I need to do when my inner critic kicks in. *Take small steps first, celebrate your wins and the "how" will eventually come into place.* My vision for the next few years seemed insane. I couldn't silence all the doubts in my mind while trying to plan it out. Here we go again: "How was I going to not just grow, but more importantly bring value to our community? How was I going to host a conference with zero budget? How was I going to find the time to get it all done?" Well, my friends, I followed this advice above, tapped into my phenomenal network and authors, learned from our community events, I pursued my curiosities to build new relationships, and the unthinkable happened. I found myself around other curious leaders that didn't just listen to my dream, but wanted to actively be part of it. Soon enough, I found them jumping in headfirst to join my vision and, in 2022, we hosted our first Leadership Summit and Book Launch of Volume 2. I'm extremely grateful to our host, University of Miami, and our corporate supporters: Hyatt, CDW, Netflix, Robertet, CareMax, Topo Chico and Fig Factor Media for believing in version 1.0 of my dream. Through their support and everyone that purchased their ticket ready to join us…this vision continues to expand. Now, when the doubts and harsh words begin to creep in, I remember to keep my heart, mind, and instinct aligned. Part of the journey is finding those who will help bridge the gap and remind me that what comes next requires taking one step forward.

THE GRAY AREA

For me, the fear of the unknown requires a fearless faith knowing that God will provide in my hardest, toughest, or darkest hours. Whether it's receiving a message through seeing a double rainbow as I type this (ask me for the picture!), my sister reassuring me "Don't worry, Pris, I've got you," or a friend that breathes affirmations into my life encouraging me not to give up, I know that God has the best plan for me and puts just the right people in my path to remind me. But as I continue on this path of self-development, my coach and my therapist have shared the same sentiment: *Priscilla, your personality & potential assessments are amazing, but confusing. You show great leadership, have lots of experiences to pull from, can genuinely connect and inspire others, but you seem to be stuck in a gray area on what's next.*

Allow me a minute to peel off my mask of looking like I "have it all together." Here is what I am really working through...what is causing this gray is my competing desire to experience motherhood. What's crazy about this is I never was that person that had a desire to be a mom, but as the years go on and a person that loves her family and friends fiercely, there is so much beauty in building your own family. As many women in their late 30s, early 40s (but let's be clear, my spirit is forever 21)...I'm at a point in my life where I love progressing in my career, but that said, I'm not oblivious that each passing year I'm running **a very close race** with my biological clock. I'm grateful to be presented with so many ideas on career choices and, up until recently, I felt that I had to choose one over the other. But why? Because *how* else would I do it all? *How* do we get to have it all? There is that *how* again ;) A fear comes over me that I'll be losing a part of myself if I go down one path over another. What do I give up and why do I give it up when all of it is me? I do not have the answers, and I am sure many of you will have much advice to give me from both sides of the coin. I've also realized that I am at a very different place than my parents were at when they had me, and while I am extremely grateful for learning through their experiences it will not help me with what we're about to go through. With the help of IVF and my amazing health benefits at CDW, I remain hopeful that someday we will welcome a healthy baby to our family. What my husband and I are about to walk through has not been done before in our family and the fear can be paralyzing and at times frustrating that I will have to figure this out…but fortunately not alone. For now, I will work towards stepping away from that fear and focus on what steps are in front of us. Working closely with my leaders to keep my career progressing, vulnerably leaning into family and friends, focusing on my curiosities, and embracing the gray. Stepping into the unknown can feel very much like walking into a dark tunnel…never-ending, blinding and full of more questions than answers. But on this journey, I am never alone…I'll be taking it one step at a time, leaning on the light of my husband, family, community and trusting in God that, yes, there are many unknowns on this path, but, in the end, "how" it will all pan out is all part of my journey.

REFLECT AND RISE

- ***Power of ONE:*** Who are you inspiring in your circle of influence? How are you moving the needle in your organization and what do the numbers say? Together we can move the needle. Here's a basic table to help you start looking at the data to see what the story is this year for your organization.

Taking Basic Pulse:	Total Latinas	% of Latinas to Total
New Hires		
Workforce		
Successors		
Turnover		

Other Data Points:
Review numbers by level
Run a Salary Analysis
Review Engagement Scores
Review BRG Data Points
Read Exit Interview Data
Launch Focus Groups

- ***Choose Action over Intention:*** Compare your numbers above to other communities in your organization to find the gaps and where to focus. Join our Latinas Rising Up In HR as a member, supporter, or sponsor and lets leverage each other to be that beacon of change. What is stopping you?

- ***One Foot Forward:*** Stop thinking about "how" you'll get that idea, goal or project done. Choose faith over fear by taking one step at a time. The doors meant for you will open and your journey will become one you never imagined.

BIOGRAPHY

Priscilla Guasso is dedicated to unlocking the keys to connections and communities. She is a talented, energetic, and driven woman who instinctively sees the potential of others and connects them to their mission by embracing their curiosities to help reveal the purposeful leader they have inside.

A skilled human resources leader, Priscilla has focused on all areas of the employee life cycle: talent acquisition, mobility, talent development, succession planning, performance management, employee relations, global diversity, equity and inclusion, and overall company culture.

With global HR experience since 2006 in the US, Latin America, Caribbean, UK, and Canada, Priscilla has spent a great deal of time in the hospitality and healthcare industries. Today, she's a proud leader on the talent management and diversity team at CDW and is an Amazon best-selling author and founder of **Latinas Rising Up In HR**®. Her passion to create actionable change is through this community of Latinas in HR and Allies, focused on one purpose: sharing their keys of knowledge and success to open doors to unlimited possibilities.

Priscilla holds a Bachelor of Science degree in business administration with a concentration in marketing from the University of Illinois, Urbana/Champaign. She is a popular and in-demand speaker known for her vulnerability and touching on topics in personal development, diversity, equity and inclusion, allyship, the power of building community, keys to networking, combating your inner critic, and embracing failure.

Based in Miami and Chicago, Priscilla enjoys traveling to new cities with her husband, Jorge, spending time with close family, salsa dancing and soaking up the sun in warmer climates.

Priscilla Guasso
HR Leader, Speaker and Author
Years in HR: 16
Info@LatinasRisingUpInHR.com
Linkedin.com/in/priscillaguasso
Instagram: @priscillaguasso @latinasinhr
www.PriscillaGuasso.com
www.LatinasRisingUpInHR.com

TRUST YOUR VALUES WILL GUIDE YOU

JOSELIN ZENEIDA SANZ

"Free and courageous people do not avoid their current circumstances, but see them as temporary."

SHIFT IN IDENTITY

I was born in a suburb of Boston but raised with my grandmother in a campo over two hours away from the capital of the Dominican Republic. My upbringing was full of love, and my grandmother was a strong woman and the first woman in my life that modeled leadership. Her leadership style was unique, and she often walked around the finca, hollering "pónganse las pilas" as she told people to get to work. It was interesting to me that her workers would simply smile and get right to it. They respected her because she led by example, and as I got older, I could credit her influence to the way she took care of her people. She was providing a way for the community to feed their families, and she shared her resources with those with less access to them. By four years old, I knew that I wanted to be a leader like her, I just had to find my own way of modeling leadership that was authentic to me.

My twin sister, Roselin, and I moved back to the US with our parents and started second grade taking ESL classes. A bus would pick us up and take us to a school on the other side of town where the ESL teacher worked. My essential classes were with a small group of students that looked like me, but for activities such as gym, art, and music, it was a different story. My classmates and I were the outsiders every time we stepped into the room. It was the first time I felt different, and that manifested itself into feeling insecure and never raising my hand in class. Those next years were a journey of navigating a new culture and understanding and accepting my own identity and how it fits in the environment I was brought into.

OVERCOMING ADVERSITY

I always knew I wanted to help people and hoped to own a business one day, but I struggled to find my "one thing." After graduating high school, I enrolled at a local university and began pursuing a bachelor's degree in Economics with a minor in Business Administration. Life was going according to plan until six months after starting college. While at work, I received a call that changed my life forever. My mom was on the other line crying as I learned she had been detained and faced immigration issues. By then my parents had been separated for over five years, so my dad was not very active in my life. I still remember standing in the hallway and dropping to my knees as the fear and uncertainty overtook me. Roselin and I were eighteen years old, while my younger brother, Bryant, was only nine years old. We considered moving Bryant to the Dominican Republic to be with her but didn't want him to miss out on potential opportunities from living in the US, so we decided to keep him with us and raise him to the best of our ability. We also had support from my dad, who picked Bryant up every other weekend and helped us financially. We took on the responsibility because at the time, his lifestyle and workload was not conducive to raising a child on his own.

My sister and I are best friends, who, through a shared mindset, were able to push each other to persevere together. We adjusted to navigating an atypical family dynamic, assuming the parent role for our brother and emotionally supporting our mom from a different country. I would often daydream on what it would be like to spontaneously go out for dinner with my mom and siblings. I missed not having her close, but I had to operate by faith, knowing better days were sure to come. I focused on diverting my energy into personal development and strategically positioning myself for success. I made a decision that I would change my family tree and have the freedom I needed to bring my family together once more.

INTRO TO HR

I worked as a bank teller while in college and was excited to finally be in close proximity to learn about money. I recognized that building relationships with the customers was my strength and sales was not, but I was still unsure of what my next step would be. One day, I attempted to contact human resources for a verification of employment. The interaction planted a seed of curiosity in me to learn more about HR and its functions. When the bank launched a mentorship program, I signed up and was paired with a recruiter. I was two months away from graduation and I had discovered the world of HR. I quickly found an internship supporting a recruiter eight hours a week, and the internship became the catalyst to landing my first HR role. It was 2013, the economy was down, and it was hard to find a job. But through networking, the same company that once hired me as a high school student offered me a role at the front desk of their HR department. I spent time studying the HR Managers and was in awe of how they effortlessly asked the right questions, interpreted what was happening, and made informed recommendations. I felt if I could learn the right decision-making principles, then I'd be able to apply it to solve problems in the future. I continued diversifying my experience and worked at two different employers before one day being laid off. It was 2016, and I was at a crossroads. My experience touched different areas within HR, but I wanted to have more depth experience in one area. Getting laid off from the private sector company led me to apply for a temporary position within a university. I covered overlapping maternity leaves for the HR Coordinator and HR Business Partner, and throughout my appointment, I acquired new skills and participated in projects I had never been a part of in the past. I was fortunate to gain mentorship and exposure to higher-level responsibilities through this role. The layoff proved to be a blessing that helped redirect my career with the specialization I was looking for.

STEPPING OUTSIDE MY COMFORT ZONE

As you rise in your HR career, you may reach a point where you can no longer hide behind a manager or your department. You must stand behind your decisions and communicate them clearly; that is where leadership grows. The spring of 2020 started a global pandemic, and by the summer the world was full-blown chaos. The gruesome murder of George Floyd triggered a global string of protests over the racism Black and African Americans experience in this country. It was a few days after the tragic incident and we had a recurring all-staff meeting at work. The burning question in my mind was whether anyone would say anything about what was going on outside of work. I felt distraught as a person, let alone as a professional. I contemplated what I could say but instantly became the shy little girl too scared to speak up. After the meeting, an employee emailed me expressing disappointment for the lack of acknowledgement from leadership about US current events surrounding racial injustice. I finally realized I needed to be the vulnerable leader that I wanted to see. I was relieved to have allies around this topic and spent the next months promoting safe spaces for conversations and listening, as well as coordinating education around racism, power, and microaggressions. The support from those that leaned in with me helped carve the way for me to gain confidence in leading. The role proved to be the most challenging, but where I felt I made the greatest impact. As HR professionals, we have direct opportunities to communicate and advocate what employees are truly feeling. This unique opportunity is fostered by getting to know your employees and building trust, understanding where their strengths lie and how to best position them for success. Their individual success will result in inevitable success for the company, and leadership will notice.

Today, I work as an HR Generalist specializing in immigration, raising my one-year-old daughter and reaping the benefits from building in my twenties. Roselin and I each have our individual homes as well as an investment property that our brother lives in. He has grown to be a respectful young man navigating his own path and is in his second year of college. As for me, after many years of putting others before myself, honoring my goals is at the top of my priority list. I don't regret my journey as a first-generation Latina who carried the responsibility to give back to my family for all the sacrifices they made. I am grateful for those experiences and the lessons because it made me the person I am today. Regardless of the setbacks, I recognize the privilege in having access to opportunities that those before me did not. I hope my story inspires you to walk by faith knowing you have the power to visualize and manifest the life that you want independent of your present circumstances.

REFLECT AND RISE

With education, support, and perseverance, we can rise up from temporary circumstances and live free and courageous lives.

1. Get clear on the skills you want to master and seek support through mentorship, training, and community to gain insight and confidence.

2. Remember, with perseverance you become unstoppable, and you have the power to build a new story and chapter for your future.

BIOGRAPHY

Joselin Sanz has leveraged her interpersonal skills and business acumen within the higher education industry to be a catalyst for change within organizations, interfacing with leadership to understand business needs and translate those needs into results and strategic human capital decisions. Joselin's ten years of progressive HR experience extends to recruiting, performance management, immigration, organizational development, and compensation. Joselin is passionate about building inclusive spaces and thrives in atmospheres taking action to be in alignment with their values.

Joselin Zeneida Sanz
HR Generalist
Years in HR: 10
joselinzsanz@gmail.com
Linkedin.com/in/joselin-sanz/

BREAKING THROUGH LIMITED BELIEFS

ANGÉLICA HERRERA-LÓPEZ

"Thriving as a first-generation Latina and finding my voice."

Having self-talks can be frightening and rewarding, but both results require deep internal digging. Growing up in Little Village, Chicago, I witnessed how the cultural norms as a first-generation Latina greatly impacted my self-esteem. I had no idea how easy it was to be swept up in the current of harmful generational cycles. As I grew, I realized how crucial it was to unlearn them in order to do better for myself, my family, and my career.

After graduating high school, I thought I was working smart by holding two jobs at a factory and in retail. I wanted to contribute an income to help my parents as a feeble attempt to compensate for all their sacrifices. Sadly, I knew that was not what they had in mind for me. My parents wanted me to go further in life, but they did not know that I struggled with confidence and held on to a limiting belief that I could not unlearn. I felt guilty for not being able to reflect my appreciation for my family with good grades, awards, or scholarships. Frankly, I felt hopeless very early on.

I took on what I believed to be a better job in catering, making deliveries in downtown Chicago. I thought that was such a great next step until I ran into a few friends from high school working corporate jobs in the administrative field. I remember feeling vulnerable when I was asked about my goals, even though I know they meant well. I couldn't share how I felt and, instead, smiled and said I enjoyed this type of work. A couple of years went by before I finally decided to go back to school to obtain a certificate as an administrative assistant. I'll never forget the smile on my dad's face when I shared the news. It made him and my mom so proud. I even remember when my mom came home from her job at an oil company and said, "Guess what? I shared with everyone that you have an office job!" Once again, I thought I had reached my potential, but that was only temporary.

A few years later, I married Eduardo and had my two sons, Eduardo and John Paul. While working as an administrative assistant and participating in many strategic planning meetings, I realized that my potential in obtaining higher roles was becoming even more limited because I did not have a degree. I was taking on more responsibilities and, yet again, I struggled, thinking that I should be grateful for the position I held, as I had already broken barriers by being in the corporate world. I decided to silence those desires and focused on raising my sons. But when my inner voice consistently reminded me of my desire to grow, I struggled to silence it and thought it was selfish of me to want to develop professionally now that I was a working mom. I did not have or see Latina role models climbing up the ladder in the company I was at and thought I should feel fulfilled.

I was never able to share those goals because I thought my time had passed. The inner critic wanted to keep me safe. To add on more, I grew up modeling my mom on how she would always ask my dad for permission before contemplating making any decision. In many ways, I repeated the cycle. It was part of my upbringing and something I viewed as normal, while silently protesting on the inside. I felt uncertain of telling my husband that I wanted to return to school, as I knew how important it was to focus on raising our family. He is very traditional and, although my culture is beautiful, I feel it is biased against women. I waited and finally had the courage to ask him for permission to return to school. It was a big financial and time commitment. In a way, part of myself wanted him to say no in order for me to, once again, silence my voice, and, indeed, he said the timing was not good. I felt defeated, but somehow, I was fine with that decision, though my soul was not. That evening, my inner voice reminded me that I needed to take risks and the time was now.

Something was changing inside of me, and I knew that if I continued with the same mentality, allowing fear to take control, I would never be able to reach my potential. Perfect timing does not exist. I felt lost, as I could not find the right balance to manage working full-time, while being present as much as possible in the boys' school activities like being the classroom mom, going on field trips, and managing my own schoolwork. I was questioning if the time commitment in each area was somehow a reflection of the quantity of my love, and I wanted someone to help me calm the mountain of doubt. In reality, I wanted to feel supported, but I didn't share these emotions with my husband, as he had warned me that it would be a lot to handle. It was then I decided to start therapy during my lunch break every week. My therapist helped me work on my anxiety, self-esteem, inner child wounds, and getting to the root of the guilt. I didn't share that I was in therapy with my family because of it being a taboo subject. The one time I did share, I was asked if I had lost faith or distanced myself from my religion. I was the coordinator and lector for Spanish mass at church for five years, and that comment hurt me. I was breaking patterns and getting to know myself, which has been one of the biggest self-care investments.

After some time, I used a planner to create a three-year strategic plan using the same model that I had used at work, but this time it was for my professional development with deadlines, budget allocation, and lots of self-determination. The goals I set for myself were scary, but this time I was determined to push through, no longer quietly working and doing it with pride. I decided to go back to school part-time while working full-time and raising my family. I remember using my train time to read, reaching out to teachers for extra support, and working late at night to finish my research papers; it was a roller coaster of emotions as some of the materials in my quantitative literacy class were a bit challenging to grasp. I was on the right track and received recognition as a member of the Alpha Sigma Lambda National Honor Society; my husband and boys attended the awards ceremony and I remember feeling so hopeful and strong. Their presence fueled me as I felt a high level of determination as I was working on providing a better future for us. In 2014, I proudly graduated with a bachelor's degree in organizational leadership from Roosevelt University with honors.

Obtaining my degree gave me confidence to obtain new positions, and I felt more fulfilled. I was promoted to office manager, assisted with HR responsibilities, and after fifteen years with the same company, I decided to expand my wings and focus on the field of HR. I joined United Airlines in the HR department. Was it scary? Very!

Was it worth it? Absolutely! This time I knew I could no longer wait years to contemplate making decisions, as life taught me to be wiser. I've held various positions in HR departments, including total rewards, talent acquisition, DEI, and Sr. HR business partner. The inner critic is always going to be part of me, but I have the right to silence it and allow my voice to remind me of the wings I have—the wings we all have, yes, you!

Every accomplishment has been loaded with fear, doubt, and a mountain of hard work, including internal work to release limiting beliefs. It didn't stop the internal struggles and I continued to focus on areas that I needed to develop as I grew in my HR position. I began working with a voice coach, Tracy Goodwin, who is the founder of Psychology of the Voice. We worked on speaking with confidence, slowing down, and speaking from a place as if the outcome is already mine. She helped me understand that I don't have to speak with sophisticated/big words, as the power comes from our tone; I used to speak so fast and didn't know it was connected to an old belief that I did not want to take time from others. Her work was magic because it helped me grow professionally and use the most powerful instrument that we have, our voice. I always proudly celebrate every accomplishment with my husband, sons, and my beautiful mom; we cry a lot together as I always remind her I owe it to her resilience and positivity. My mom gives me strength. She only finished the first grade of grammar school in Mexico, but the changes she's made as we've both become more resilient has made us stronger and bolder, mi madrecita hermosa. When I mentor others, I point to my experiences as an example that growth is not always linear.

I continued to work diligently to obtain my SHRM-CP, SHRM People Manager Qualification credential, and was appointed as Member of the Emerging Professionals Advisory Council (EPAC) for SHRM and committed mentor. I've become a lifelong learner and have attended four SHRM conferences and SHRM Inclusion conferences to deepen my HR knowledge. I consistently set professional development goals each quarter and know there are no limits. I graduated from the Mujeres de HACE Women's Leadership program and have become a facilitator empowering our community.

Time passes by very fast! My sons are now teenagers; Eduardo is a freshman in college and John Paul is a sophomore in high school. I occasionally ask them for their input as I take on new challenges, and when they respond with such positive encouragement, it's so rewarding. They remind me to stay focused when I want to skip my reading as I prepare for my SHRM-SCP exam this fall.

Giving back is so important and rewarding on so many levels. I'm honored to be able to manage the United-Year Up partnership program mentoring and working with diverse young adults, supporting their internship growth with the goal of having 80 percent to be hired at United. I share my experiences with them and fully invest in their development as I see myself in them, focusing on the importance of creating a safe space, empowering them to reach their full potential, and have a fair opportunity. I want everyone to know that it takes hard work, but we are each truly resilient.

We're all born with special wings. Sometimes our wings get clipped along the way, but never forget we have it within us to grow stronger, to set goals, conquer, seek others for help, and know there are no limits, only hard work. When I was younger, I remember watching the airplanes in the sky, so far away, and never imagined that one day I would be making a positive impact in people's lives at United Airlines. In our travels, we can get to different destinations from different airports. The same is true in life: our journeys are different, but the dreams are there, and all it takes is for you to tap into your inner child to reveal what aspirations are keeping you up at night.

Finally, I can say in the open that I'm a confident, strong, Latina Rising Up In HR, and I truly hope my story has inspired you. *¡Sí se puede!*

REFLECT AND RISE

As a Latina, we have to work harder to achieve our goals because of our cultural norms and lack of support.

It is never too late to accomplish your dreams, continue to persevere, and live your truth.

Don't underestimate your value and past sacrifices; growth truly begins at the end of your comfort zone.

Changing the way we think is not a switch and requires a lot of work. It takes a lot of self-exploration and investment.

We were raised to believe what others told us, what rules and roles we were supposed to follow, and that is sometimes harmful.

Honor yourself and be proud to showcase your wins.

BIOGRAPHY

Angélica Herrera-López, SHRM-CP, is a Sr. Human Resources professional with over eight years of strong HR experience. She's a Sr. HR Business Partner at United Airlines. Angélica is first-generation Mexican American. She earned her bachelor's degree in organizational leadership from Roosevelt University and obtained her SHRM-CP in 2018.

She is committed to her professional development, has volunteered at the SHRM Conferences as session host, and enjoys giving back to the community. Angélica graduated from the Mujeres de HACE Leadership program in July 2021 and is passionate about diversity, leadership, and all areas in HR. She is the proud mom of Eduardo and John Paul Lopez.

Angélica Herrera-López, SHRM-CP
Senior Human Resources Partner
Years in HR: 8+
angielopez0212@gmail.com
Linkedin.com/in/angieherreralopez/

YO SOY. I AM.

ARLENE NAIRN

"Be a person of worth, not just a person of success."

MATRIARCHAL DESCENT

Today, I stand grateful and humbled as a Corporate Director of Human Resources. I remind myself that I am more than a title; I am also someone's daughter and granddaughter. I am a Latina, a friend, and a survivor. I am also a faith believer and a woman who is constantly growing both personally and professionally. I am a work in progress. How did I get here? I owe my current blessings to my beautiful warrior, my abuelita, Dr. Esther Basurto. Also, I owe so much to the strongest woman I know, my mother, Ingrid Nairn, who has a master's degree in International Business. I come from a strong line of powerful female pioneers who have always taught me the value of women in society, and I am very proud to carry that message every day of my life.

I was born in Hollywood, Los Angeles, California. Being a forward thinker, my mom decided I should be born in the United States, where I would have a better future and be free to live my best life. She got pregnant at the age of nineteen back when women still had the right to choose. My mom chose to give me the best life she could—but it did not come easy for her. At six months old, the doctors told her that I would never be able to walk, and I was put in a cast from my chest down to the rest of my little body for almost a year. My mom has told me that my life at this point was full of tears and pain from the blisters that the cast caused. Thankfully, and after many years of physical therapy, I was able to walk properly. Meanwhile, my mother worked the graveyard shift at LAX, and my abuelita worked in Compton, California, as an English professor. She sent us money for medical expenses, and though we lived in a one-bedroom apartment with only a mattress on the floor and the bare essentials, my childhood was always full of love.

We moved several times all across Mexico. I grew up chasing sheep, feeding the bunnies, pigs, and peacocks, and milking the cows every morning at four o' clock in Hidalgo, Mexico. I was six years old when we moved to Baja California, Mexico to live in my Abuelita's home. It was then that I also got my first job selling roses at a gas station. I was eight years old when my mom enrolled me in school in Calexico, California, USA, where I started to learn English. The commute to school with Abuelita is one of my favorite memories. On our drive to the US border, she would make me recite all my prayers, the English verb tenses, and the times table. If I made a mistake, when I got home, I would have to write it down one hundred times. Thank you for teaching me discipline and work ethic, Abuelita.

BECOMING A SURVIVOR

Let me preface that this part of my story from many years ago was once a painful and closed chapter unbeknownst to many. My intention with opening it back up is to help make sure history doesn't repeat itself with other young women in our community and to share that there is light in this dark world...you are not alone. I am also reminding myself that I am no longer a victim but a survivor with a powerful and thriving voice. Without going into too much detail, I had a turbulent childhood. If I did not have faith, the kind of faith my Abuelita taught me, I don't think I would have had the resilience and strength to keep going. When I was young, someone close thought it was acceptable for me to endure abuse and for many years, I thought it was my fault, that I was the one to blame. I thought that I was responsible for this horrible person stealing my happiness, my innocence, and my childhood. As I've healed, I realize now how I spent two decades unnecessarily angry at myself and believing I was not a worthy person. I did say no to protect myself, but I was ignored. My voice was silenced, and my will was violated. We live in a society where speaking about trauma can be taboo; it makes people uncomfortable. But I can assure you that talking about it with the right people and getting the right help has freed me from guilt and pain. Coming forward as a survivor is extremely difficult. You put yourself out there to be judged, criticized, and shamed. This is why a lot of survivors don't come forward and the vicious cycle continues. I ask that you not feel sorry for me or think "Wow, pobrecita." I've been able to move forward because I feel I have a personal responsibility to advocate for those that can't. I will continue to speak out about the power of saying NO and the powerful transformation of becoming a survivor. Why? Because you matter, you are enough, and once you heal, you will be that ray of light in someone else's darkness.

I have nothing but gratefulness and pride for my mother, who raised me alone with very limited resources. She had such strength to walk away and fight for a better future for the both of us. My mom met Peter when I was eleven years old. He is the love of her life, her best friend, and the most loving, caring, funny, and respectful husband and father a girl could ask for. Peter adopted me, gave me a family, a home, and two incredible siblings, Peter and Andrew, who inspire me every single day. I love you, brothers, and I am so proud of both of you. It was through their love and vision for a future family that I could finally say goodbye to being alone, no longer fearing that one-bedroom apartment with just a mattress on the floor. My dad changed my world for the better, my perspective in life, and shaped me into the strong, independent woman I am—thank you, Dad.

FEARLESS AND UPWARD

While in college in San Diego, I worked as a night auditor for Hyatt hotels from 10:00 p.m. to 6:30 a.m. There, I was given the opportunity to attend a selective leadership program led by my dearest friend and mentor, Sonya Lamas. I was then promoted to Housekeeping and Pool Supervisor. While working in this position, I would visit the human resources office where Sonya worked, bringing donuts and coffee for everyone in the office. I wanted them to know me because I didn't want to continue cleaning bird poop from pool chairs every day; instead, I wanted to become a trustworthy resource to all my employees. I wanted to show that I was capable of more. I just needed someone to believe in me. I had been preparing for this opportunity since I sold roses at the gas station all those years ago. Sonya Lamas believed in me and recommended me for a Human Resources Coordinator position with Doug Sullivan. He hired me and made me part of his team—thank you for believing in me, Doug. Little did I know that I was heading into the best opportunity because of these two outstanding leaders.

Over the next three years, I was promoted four times, and ultimately, found myself in Los Angeles. During my time with Hyatt, I found my passion; I was the voice for not only minorities but encouraged all employees to speak up, to find their voice. I was fearless and fought for equality, honesty, fairness, and professional growth.

MY CHOICE

In December of 2020, I was recruited by my current employer and brought my knowledge, my love for human resources, and my work ethic to Luxe Hotels. This change has been a unique and blessed opportunity. I have created a culture of respect, with good work ethic, and a fun environment! Being Latina has made me stand out and be noticed.

For many of us, we don't realize how hard we've been working, or how truly exhausted we are until someone stands behind us and offers to catch us. I have felt this pressure for much of my life. This is why I am so passionate about the well-being of each one of my colleagues. I counsel people who feel out of place and I always make time to listen to those who need a sprinkle of inspiration or mentorship. I have continuously progressed in my career and met every challenge as an opportunity to make a difference, to learn, and to thrive. I am so grateful that I did not have to stop working through the pandemic, but it was far from easy. My decision to be married to my job comes at a relatively high cost. While I love what I do, I have put my personal life on hold many times to ensure I do not disappoint anyone at work or my friends and family. Now, I am focused on my personal growth and I remind myself every day to be kind with my mind and body. I also remind myself to have compassion for the young Arlene who lives in me. I strive to make her proud of all my accomplishments while reminding myself to forgive and trust.

Reflecting back, I see that, no matter how many challenges have come into my life, the constant variable has been determination while being fearless with an unstoppable work ethic! I'm strong, resilient, and caring while sometimes cynical and overbearing. I recognize when I'm not yet at my fullest potential, but I adjust to whatever life throws at me so that I may continue to experience growth. My journey is about healing and giving myself permission to take up space and to gracefully take care of myself. I am grateful for all the life lessons, especially the ones that seemed most difficult. We are never done; there is always more to do or another person to help. I'm not done. I will continue to go out there and wrestle for what I want and deserve—this is my time.

*Special gratitude goes to my mother, my wellness coaches, my friends, and lastly, my Abuelita. To this day, she continues to be a warrior for everyone, even when she can't stand on her own. Abuelita, your love will forever be my safety net. I dedicate my story to you.

REFLECT AND RISE

I've never been like an ostrich; I was never one to stick my head in the sand. On the contrary, I want to leave a mark, advocate for change, especially for those who need a voice. I'm okay with the fact that sometimes, doing the right thing gets ugly.

Keep being assertive

Keep on leading

Keep telling the truth

Keep taking up space

Keep asking hard questions

Keep being vulnerable, honest, and kind

BIOGRAPHY

Arlene Nairn is a Corporate Director of Human Resources who earned her degree from San Diego State University. Her educational background is in administration; her professional background is in Human Resources; both gave her structure and organization to be a quick thinker and problem solver. Human resources taught her so much about people and relationships. Her intuitive nature and ability to read people have allowed her to make connections and build meaningful relationships.

She enjoys volunteering her time for nonprofit organizations like MakeAWish, Hands4Hope LA, and Ronald McDonald House. She is passionate about building relationships between Hispanic communities, and as an author for *Latinas Rising Up In HR*, she speaks about her journey to try and support other women to realize they deserve every opportunity to step into their full potential. Arlene received a Special Commendation from the Human Relations Commission and she is going back to school to further her education. Arlene's desire is to inspire and empower others to achieve greatness in their life.

Arlene Nairn
Corporate Director of Human Resources
Years in HR: 8
nairnarlene@gmail.com
Linkedin.com/in/arlene-nairn-41286545/

PONIÉNDOME LAS PILAS

VANESSA DURÁN

"Rising above with fearless determination, a personal board of directors, and a little bit of luck."

INTRODUCTION

It's a muggy Miami evening and I am enjoying a St. Germain spritz on a high-rise rooftop. I just closed another complex workplace investigation and my mind is weary. The sun is setting and I am taking in the views of the twinkling cosmopolitan below me before I submit the final draft of this essay. As I skim it one last time, I am letting myself feel every little emotion—vulnerability, pride, anxiety, and finally, catharsis. Statistics probably indicate that I am not supposed to reach these heights, literally and figuratively.

I was the firstborn child to two teen parents. My family came to the United States in the late 1980s and I did not speak English until age six. I overcame socioeconomic barriers and secured admission into the number-one public university in the United States. I also managed to carve out a corporate career at the intersection of people, employment law, and business despite my belonging being called into question at many points along the way.

"OVERMATCHED" WITH UCLA

I matriculated at UCLA in the 2010s. My academic journey was plagued by a common demon that a lot of first gens struggle to overcome in higher education: impostor syndrome. When I was an undergraduate, a professor published a study criticizing affirmative action, which labeled students of color from disadvantaged backgrounds as "overmatched" with prestigious institutions of higher education. I was not alone in feeling like I was being told that I did not deserve my place at UCLA. I latched on to that feeling of otherness for a significant part of my undergraduate experience.

I also found myself growing resentful of my privileged peers that comfortably relied on their families to pay for their education, while the guilt of asking mine to stretch their limited resources led me to juggle multiple part-time jobs at once to cover housing and other basic expenses. Often, it felt like I was struggling to shoulder the weight of my academic and work commitments. I became despondent when I saw my GPA dip below 3.0.

Thanks to scholarships I had accumulated, I was eventually able to sustain one part-time job. I used the extra breathing room to bulk up on courses that focused on law, labor, and the Latinx experience in the US. I learned about the sociopolitical and economic barriers that framed my community's experience, and my transcripts reflected that I was engaging with and retaining the material. *Me puse las pilas* and I achieved a 3.56 grade point average during my junior and senior years.

UNCONVENTIONAL NETWORKING & FALLING INTO HR

Like many other young adults, I had no idea what career I wanted to pursue after graduation. Like the rest of my peers, I was also active on dating apps.

The summer after graduation, I matched with an MBA student at UCLA Anderson who asked about my career plans. I disclosed that I originally wanted to go to law school and become an employment or immigration attorney, but the financial commitment was not sensible at that time. I was mentally and physically exhausted from my efforts to self-fund the degree I had just obtained. So, I decided to put that aspiration on hold, enjoy Los Angeles a little longer, and take time to determine if this was truly an area I wanted to commit to.

He connected me with a friend who worked at an

entertainment studio that had an opening for a Human Resources Assistant. As it turned out, this mutual friend was a member of a cross-town chapter of my sorority. I saw an opportunity, *me puse las pilas* once again, and I jump-started my career in HR. I went through the hiring process, and while I did not have any prior internship experience, I think the hiring team recognized my extraordinary drive and work ethic. They saw potential, and ultimately, I was hired.

NAVIGATING THE CORPORATE WORKPLACE

My professional experience continuously nurtured my passion for exploring the intersections of business, people, and law. While working in the aerospace industry, I was part of a team that eliminated 10 percent of the workforce during a period of financial uncertainty. One of my specific contributions to this unfortunate project involved consulting with impacted Spanish speakers that suddenly had to navigate outplacement resources and complex unemployment systems. I learned that people have increased difficulty reconciling business decisions with their new realities when they cannot access a trusted, competent HR professional that can interpret the law in plain language. I saw my parents and elders in those impacted individuals and did my best to leave them with a thorough understanding of their options as they transitioned out.

At other points in my career, I have had to rise above workplace bullies, office politics, microaggressions, and bad supervisors. There is no playbook in existence that tells us exactly what to do when faced with these challenges, but these situations are particularly vexing for first-generation professionals that cannot lean on family members or neighbors for advice when navigating corporate workplace norms and expectations. One key to overcoming impostor syndrome for me when it tried to creep in at work was to lean on my personal board of directors—that close network of peers and cross-functional partners with different areas of expertise—to remind me of my value.

Some of the best mentors I have ever had were senior peers that saw value in my contributions when I was in the weeds with a project that streamlined the employee experience. Your supervisor cannot be everywhere all at once, and any performance evaluations they deliver will largely consist of their own limited experiences working with you. I have worked at organizations without formal systems for collecting 360 assessments, and in those environments, opportunities for professional growth hinged on how often your customers and teammates had positive feedback about you.

One of my favorite former colleagues used to send occasional emails to my direct supervisor, who was frequently tucked away in their office, to highlight the hard work

I put in that week. She would blind copy me on that initial correspondence, and on particularly hard weeks where my contributions did not feel seen, I would revisit those notes and press forward. There is privilege here too. I am lucky to have worked with people that recognized my potential, invested in my development, and advocated for me without expecting anything in return. This approach to recognition built mutual trust with my senior peers and opened my eyes to a leadership style that I hope to emulate.

A significant number of the Spanish-speaking employees I have interacted with throughout the first decade of my career have expressed frustration with the inaccessibility of US employment law, difficulty adapting to cultural work norms, and understanding reporting procedures for grievances.

I often find that nuestra gente are underserved in corporate environments, particularly in the HR space, due to the short supply of Spanish-speaking business professionals. If you have ever tried to translate a legal document for a family member, only for their fear and confusion to take over and ask you, "*¿Entonces para qué te mandamos a la escuela?*" then I urge you to consider a future in human resources. As a child, one feels inept when met with this response. But as someone who has revisited these conversations as an adult, I can tell you that nuestros padres wear their fear and discomfort on their sleeve when they approach someone for help in a bright, open-concept corporate office. They are unsure of the kind of response they will be met with or if there will even be someone available that can speak their language. Your Spanish-speaking skills are desperately needed in these spaces.

ENCONTRANDO MI CAMINO

I have since shifted to a critical HR subspecialty: workplace investigations of harassment, discrimination, and retaliation. The COVID-19 pandemic has shown us that the workplace can change in the blink of an eye. With continuing education becoming more crucial than ever, I set my sights on obtaining professional certificates and credentials through institutions like HRCI and the Association of Workplace Investigators.

Ultimately, my career trajectory led me back to my original ambition of attending law school, though not for a juris doctor. You see, working with attorneys taught me that practicing the law is not like what you see on *Law & Order*. My interest in employment law remained constant, but the gap years I took in my twenties and the networking I engaged in revealed that I would not find fulfillment in being a litigator. I thought that the only way to obtain a legal education was through a JD program for much of my first decade in HR. I have since learned of alternatives like Master of Legal Studies and Dispute Resolution degrees that still nurture this interest in the law without an expected path to licensure.

I strive to be the professional development resource I did not have when I was a student and early career professional. In sharing my experience, I offer a glimpse into the pressing need for more Spanish-speaking professionals in the HR space. I also hope to continue to prove that those of us who come from disadvantaged backgrounds can go on to have careers every bit as successful as our privileged counterparts.

We are in a unique position to be of particular service to members of our communities by making the rules of employment and our professional spaces more accessible and less intimidating. We need more Latinas within executive levels of the HR function. It's time for us to answer the call and rise.

REFLECT AND RISE

- **Some individuals may question or undermine your existence in higher education and corporate spaces where strategic decisions are made.** These people fail to consider that strategic networking, hard work, and leaning on your personal board of directors more than makes up for whatever disadvantage you may have risen from.

- **Good people look out for other good people.** The best mentors (and organizations) will see value in your potential and invest in your success. As you gain momentum in your career, be that person for others without expecting anything in return. If a peer or cross-functional customer made a significant contribution, recognize them by sending a quick note to their team lead. Wins and achievements do not always get the same attention as dropped balls often do.

- **Recognize a valuable networking opportunity and seize it.** No, I am not telling you to blast your résumé on dating apps. However, when your casual conversations organically veer in that direction, seize the opportunity and pay it forward the next time someone could use a hand.

BIOGRAPHY

Based in Los Angeles and Miami, Vanessa Durán is an HR professional with seven years of experience across the entertainment, aerospace, and fitness industries. A proud double Bruin, she is working toward an MLS in Legal Studies from UCLA Law and holds a BA in Political Science and Labor & Workplace Studies. She finds professional fulfillment in discerning systemic trends and making organizational recommendations that proactively manage risk. Vanessa thrives in environments where HR practitioners and senior business leaders partner pragmatically to transform the employee experience, continuously drive efficiency, and achieve business goals. She enjoys traveling to new cities with her partner, Austin, and is on a mission to take a SoulCycle class in every market.

Vanessa Durán
Employee Relations Specialist
Years in HR: 7
vanessaduranlopez@gmail.com
Linkedin.com/in/vanessaduranlopez/

STRENGTH & PERSEVERANCE - IT'S IN OUR BLOOD

BRENDA SÁNCHEZ-PINEDA

"Don't forget where you came from while never losing sight of where you are going."

STAY THE COURSE

When I reflect on the beginning of my career in HR, I'm truly in disbelief of how I got through the journey so far. I was living on my own and attending college for my bachelor's degree in Psychology when I got my first job in HR. I was the assistant to the VP of Human Resources at a Fortune 500 company in Manhattan, and I felt like the luckiest girl in the world. It was my first corporate job, and I was the first one in my family to have one. (Not to mention the first one in my family to go to college.) What a feeling!

I had come from a nonprofit organization in East Harlem where I worked as the Executive Assistant to the

Executive Director of the organization. I started school while I was there and received tuition reimbursement for one class per semester. Yes. One class per semester. I decided I would pay for one class while the organization would pay for the other. It was all I could afford at that time. I remember the ED coming to see me with the approval form in his hand. He had doubts about how serious I was about my education based on this plan. I explained to him that it was simply all I could afford at the time. It took me ten years to complete my bachelor's degree in Psychology. It felt longer than it turned out. The years were going to go by anyway. I figured before I knew it, I would be done. I kept a goal calendar and checked off my courses as I completed them. By the time I finished undergraduate school, I had been in my HR Administrative Assistant role in Corporate America for six years.

I knew I would eventually return to school for my graduate degree in Human Resources Management. Why wouldn't I? I was now part of a corporate HR team supporting the VP of Human Resources. But I felt like I needed a break after ten years. A small break. That was all I wanted. Maybe one semester off. A year and a half later, my VP of HR asked me for the fourth or fifth time when I was returning to grad school. I finally bit the bullet and registered at the Milano Graduate School of The New School University (now The New School). That fall, I started my graduate program, and for three years did it all over again.

CARPE DIEM!

During my Immigration and Recruiting specialist role, I was invited to the annual National Society of Hispanic MBA (NSHMBA) event in Orlando, Florida. As a Latina with a master's degree, I was specifically chosen to represent the company! At the same time, I had been working on an international transfer to the US Sales Organization to fill an open sales manager role. I partnered with the HR Manager for that client group on the visa process, and spoke with her weekly. She was located in Atlanta, GA, and I worked out of the New York office, so I had never met her in person. To my surprise, the HR Manager was also at NSHMBA, and lo and behold, she was recruiting for an HR Generalist to help her support the Sales organization. What!? I immediately looked at her and said, "Throw my name in the hat." She spoke to the right people (including her direct supervisor, who was 100 percent on board!), pulled a couple of people together, and the stars must have been aligned that week, because everyone that needed to be there was there. I was offered the HR Generalist role at the end of the event, and when I returned to New York, I started working with the HR Manager in supporting the Sales organization!

My very first meeting with the Sales team was in Pasadena, California. I was up early and ready by 7 a.m. I wanted to make a great impression on my new manager and the infamous sales team. As I walked down the hall toward the meeting room, I could hear laughing, singing, and loud music. All I could think was, *Who are these people making all this noise so early in the morning right before a work meeting?!* When I opened the door, there were 150 sales managers. Dressed up and ready to take on the world! I could not believe the energy in that room. It was amazing. I immediately took to the group and spent the next three days learning about their roles and their challenges. My manager and I debriefed and worked for days to come up with ways to help them overcome the obstacles that were keeping them from meeting their goals. I wanted to witness whatever stumbling blocks they came across for myself, so I spent time in the field with them. It was the only way I could truly understand what they needed and how I could help the business provide these resources.

It was during my time supporting US Sales that I learned how important relationships are for business. As the Sales HR Generalist, I served as backup to the other three HRMs on the team. After one of those managers could no longer cover two client groups, I stepped in and I was promoted to HR Manager for the Sales Organization. I was so excited, I could not contain myself! It wasn't how I expected to get my first promotion, but things don't always come to you the way you think. I had to embrace it, and I did! I could not wait to get started as a true HR

Business Partner for my group. I made every effort to attend all of their meetings. I wanted to sit around the table with them. I wanted to be part of their team so that we could brainstorm new ways to grow the business. Most importantly, I wanted to get to know the talent on the team. Who the strong performers were and who were the weakest links. It wouldn't stop there. There would have to be a backup plan. A plan to address performance and increase productivity across the division. Having this knowledge would give me what I needed to build my credibility with the VP of Sales. I began working closely with the sales leaders in my group and learned everyone's name, their background and experience, and who had the strongest players on their teams. Sort of like a coach—the coach knows everything about the players, and who to put in the game to score big. I help the client identify the strong performers and work together to create a robust retention and development plan to keep them.

JUMP

I supported the Sales Organization as the HRBP for over five years, when the VP of Sales called me into her office. She said, "Brenda, I want you to join my team." I was a bit confused, since I thought I already was a part of her team.

I laughed and said, "I am part of your team."

She said, "No. I want you to be part of the Sales Organization as my Sales Support Manager." This role was a huge responsibility like that of the Chief of Staff to the VP of Sales. I looked around and thought, *She must be crazy!*

I said, "Really? Me? You think I can do that job?" and she reminded me of my strengths.

She said, "Brenda, you know the business and you know my team. They love and trust you. I promise you that if you take this role in sales, you will go back to human resources as a better and stronger business partner than before." Wow! I told her I would think about it and went home in a daze. I thought to myself, *Can you really make this switch? You studied Psychology and Human Resources management for over ten years! All you have ever done has been in HR? Are you really going to jump?*

The next day I went to see the VP of Sales and said, "Sign me up!"

She was so happy. She said, "You will not regret this!" and she was right! I cannot tell you how valuable that experience was for me. For the next four years, I went on to fill additional sales roles such as Sales Project Manager, Sales Division Manager, and National Sales Operations manager. By the time I went back to HR, I had completed a full rotation in the Sales organization.

NEVER STOP LEARNING

There were so many lessons from my time in the Sales Organization. Looking at the HR function from an outside role is an experience on a different level. If you get the chance to do it—take it! It will provide you with insight to HR that you would have never been exposed to otherwise. It was an experience I took with me back to HR and will never forget.

Not only did I get to experience HR from the outside, but I had the opportunity of working alongside great leaders while gaining tons of business knowledge. Several years later, while reporting to the VP of Human Resources in another company, I was met with the chance to "jump" again. We had been talking about my promotion to Director for some months when she suddenly announced her resignation. Wait. But what about my promotion? I knew that if I was going to be promoted, I'd have to take control of it on my own. A month after the VP left, I gathered my performance reviews and a list of all my accomplishments. I met with the President/CEO and presented my case. Nervous could not begin to describe how I was feeling. I could not believe I walked into his office and asked to be promoted. He took the folder from my hand, reviewed it for about five minutes, and said "OK." Okay?! Did he just say I can be promoted… to Director? I was so excited. Before I walked out of his office, I turned around and asked, "Director, right?" I did not want there to be any confusion whatsoever.

Looking back, I can see how my confidence played a major role along the way. Recently, I found my college yearbook quote: *"Never let anything get in the way of your vision of yourself in the future."* I can thankfully say I have stuck to those words and continue to live by that mantra. I had a timeline in mind for reaching the Director role and I met it two months after the goal. But you know what? I made it, and I am not done. In my current role of Human Resources Director, I continue to learn about myself and the type of leader that I am. I find myself serving as a mentor to others in the company (in and out of HR). I think of all the times I could have used "a Brenda"—so I keep that in mind when I am coaching other young women who are early in their career or just starting their career in HR.

REFLECT AND RISE

- **Stay the course:** no matter how challenging your goals seem, do not give up. You can change them, but don't erase them. Keep at it. I went to school for ten years, and the only way I was able to get through it was tracking my courses on a calendar I kept on the refrigerator! Looked at it every day and every night…knowing there was an end.

- **Carpe diem:** Seize the moment. Be prepared and be ready. When the opportunity presents itself—speak up! Throw your hat in the ring.
- **Jump:** When it's scary and it takes you out of your comfort zone, that's when you JUMP! Strap on tight, confidence on high, then do it! You will not regret it!
- **Never stop learning:** As businesses grow, evolve, and change, so does the HR Business Partner role—they change, we change. It's how we show up.

BIOGRAPHY

With an extensive background and years of experience in supporting Sales organizations, Brenda has led strong and robust performance management processes that focus on meeting targets and increasing business growth. Brenda Sánchez-Pineda is Director of Human Resources at Robertet, Inc., a fragrance and flavor manufacturer with offices in New York, New Jersey, and Canada. She leads the first ever Diversity, Equity, and Inclusion strategy at Robertet, Inc., where she has been for five years. Prior to Robertet, Brenda held HR positions at Scholastic and Avon Products in New York City. Brenda is committed to mentoring young women in navigating life and career challenges, and volunteers her time when she can. She has a bachelor's degree in Psychology and a master's degree in Human Resources Management from the Milano Graduate School of the New School University. Brenda's thesis in graduate school was on "Leadership Styles and Gender Differences." She is bilingual of Puerto Rican descent. She loves music and spending time with her family. Brenda is married and lives in Pennsylvania with her husband, mom, and two shih tzus, Toby and Mia.

Brenda Sánchez-Pineda
Director, Human Resources
Years in HR: 20+
Brendapineda213@gmail.com
Linkedin.com/in/brenda-l-sanchez-pineda-84b1642/

RIDING THE WAVES OF CONSTANT CHANGE

ARIANA J. PAZ

"No matter how many redirections come your way, create your own reality by moving forward. Adelante siempre."

Since I was a child, I've dreamed of tall skyscrapers, offices that look out over a skyline, rising high above a bustling metropolis, and a woman rushing through it all to her desk. The career women in those early eighties movies making their way up in Corporate America never left me. As I reflect now from my Chicago high-rise, it's hard to believe my dream is a reality.

Growing up, I was constantly shifting between two worlds. I loved both dearly. It was normal for me to cross the border from my home in Del Rio, Texas, to Cuidad Acuña, Mexico, multiple times a week to visit family and friends. The two cultures were separated by the Rio Grande

River and woven into every part of my life. I embraced the unique duality as a part of who I am, both Mexican and American. Unbeknownst to me at the time, navigating these cultural crossroads and belonging to those two worlds shaped how I thought and acted. My parents left high school to devote their lives to working and caring for their family. I went to school with children whose relatives, like mine, were migrant farm workers. My maternal abuelo had a mere third-grade education and spent long days dedicated to back-breaking field work. My grandfather on my dad's side had the rare opportunity to pursue a college education. He left his doctorate program for family obligations, but I saw the change, the culture, and the opportunity that came with his higher education degrees. I embraced those two opposing worlds, two distinct cultures both driven by love, family, and dedication. As I tried to find my place, I felt education was the path to breaking barriers, and it was how I'd define myself.

Most of my classmates never dreamed of leaving the Lonestar State, and success was at most going to a nearby college in larger cities like San Antonio, Austin, or Dallas and returning home. We are Latinos, and family comes first, especially as a young woman. At times, I felt guilty for wanting more, to focus on myself and not follow the traditional route. Growing up Latina, women all around me valued home, marriage, and motherhood above all else. Family is so important to me, and it grounds me when times are hard, but I knew I had to make a hard choice to charter my own path that was opposite of the norm to achieve my dreams. Pursuing an education, and moving away from my home, not once but twice, all symbolized a sacrifice that I hoped would someday help me give back in my own way. Despite my fears, my mother also taught me to embrace my independence with grit and resilience. I knew I had her same fighting spirit, and that ultimately this would make me a stronger woman.

As I sat in my middle school classroom, I was snapped back to reality. My history teacher approached me after class. I was outgoing, really talkative, and at times, disruptive. He scolded me harshly, his words piercing me and fueling a passion deep within. He said, "Ariana, if you don't learn how to listen to others, you will end up barefoot and pregnant by eighteen!" He had just compared me to a statistic, and only saw my future as a teen mom, a dropout. More than that, he doubted my ability to listen. I took that criticism and harnessed it to propel me forward. My strong will would show him and others who never thought I'd make it far. From that point on, I wasn't just going to graduate, but I was determined to make it out of Texas, listen to others with tact and diplomacy, and rise to city skyscraper heights. It was all the motivation I needed.

CHASING THE CITY LIGHTS

After six years, I finally graduated college. I moved to San Antonio, roughly 300 miles from my family, and started at a community college before transferring to University of Texas at San Antonio. I took evening classes and studied between working full-time, navigating the path to a degree in International Business and Marketing. Then, in 2008, the recession hit. I had finally started my career at a local ad agency when I was part of a large layoff, and while I didn't know it then, my career took an important turn. I picked myself up and pushed forward, landing my first role in HR as a training and recruiting specialist. I learned how the right talent can powerfully impact an organization.

With momentum building once again and experience behind me, I couldn't shake that vision of an even bigger city. Another step I knew I needed to take and conquer. I knew there were more opportunities out there if I opened myself up to the challenge of a move, even if it meant leaving my family and friends behind for a second time. I could hear the words of my middle school teacher ring loud in my head once again, and I listened hard this time, to my heart.

After visiting Chicago, I quickly fell in love with it. Moving there became my goal, and after a couple of interviews, I got a job offer on the spot. I had to find a place to live and wondered if I'd survive the frigid Midwest winters. Within two months, I said my goodbyes and started on the path toward growing my HR career.

I didn't go to school for Human Capital Management, otherwise known as Human Resources, nor did I have any certifications tailored to the profession, but my appetite for a role beyond recruiting grew. I knew I was a quick learner and set my eyes on switching to a more strategic role. After no less than seven intimidating interviews with senior executives, I landed my first role as an HR Business Partner at a global manufacturing company. Here, over roughly five years, I gained significant opportunities to stretch my skill set and grew in ways I couldn't have envisioned. I was part of a global restructure where I learned change management methodologies and the importance of building trust with your team. I built a solid foundation and used that to step into other leadership roles at a global pharmaceutical company where I helmed HR for the US and Mexico. Traveling internationally and having a seat at the table with all white, older men is where I found my voice, and it grew louder.

THE LADDER GOES BOTH WAYS

I learned what it meant to lead a vision and dedicate personal and professional hours to getting the job done. I had a long reverse commute, with many workdays ending past 9 p.m. Still, I challenged myself to not collapse on the couch but instead dove into networking events for the Chicago HR community. This was the time. Those relationships, and a new community of resources, proved invaluable as a stepping stone in my career. You never know when and where someone will cross your path and introduce you to a new opportunity.

I was swept up in the networking and accepted a dinner meeting that turned into an enticing opportunity to lead a small operation as their first People and Culture Director. The title and the prospect of leading an uncharted path was all so attractive to me. I knew I had the experience and was prepared to hit the ground running. Unfortunately, after three short months, I was met with haunting words: I "wasn't a good fit" for the role. I was shocked! That feeling was the definition of a gut punch. I was left confused, angry, and disappointed. I had left a stable, nurturing global corporation for this. The reasoning was unclear, and as a consistent top performer in my earlier roles, I instantly felt knocked down. I questioned everything and thought, *Maybe I don't have what it takes.*

I took the time to reflect and leaned on the growing network I'd built. I had to *remember that failure is just that, an experience and redirection.* Failure, a word I hadn't let into my vocabulary, now had me wondering "How did this happen to me?" I never got the answer and I never will, but that experience made me more resilient. I soon found myself busy with interim consulting projects, until another HR leadership opportunity came knocking on my door that seemed just right. It was February 2020.

Despite the pandemic, I was able to hang on to my role for several months. I was surrounded by furloughs and layoffs, tasked with one of the hardest jobs in HR, until I, too, was let go late summer. I couldn't help but think, *Here I go again*. I felt lost in the trenches, wondering what was next as the pandemic stretched past six months. Should I move back to Texas, return to my family and my former life? While walking along the lakeshore one morning, it all became clear. I had always wanted to get my MBA, and now was the time to do it.

DEGREES OF CHANGE

The pandemic, and working from home, allowed me to manifest what I had long delayed since moving to Chicago. I had been so busy building a decade's worth of accomplishments that I hadn't made time for another major life goal. I immersed myself in a post-graduate program in Change Management at Kellstadt Graduate School of Business at DePaul University. Change was all around us, as employees and companies were pressed to evolve to stay afloat. I knew this was the step I needed to take my HR career to the next level.

Earning my MBA was an arduous process, but I'm filled with pride for the sacrifices I made to achieve this milestone, not only for me but for my family. Thinking about my over twenty cousins, tíos y tías, only three of us hold that level of degree. I thought about my younger self, struggling in middle school, and how I wanted my journey to be an example to the younger generation. Even when you face layoffs and inexplicable failure, with perseverance it is ALL possible. Having the perseverance to pursue my MBA after thinking it was too late in my career and while navigating a pandemic, it's the accomplishment I'm most proud of in my life, personally and professionally.

I feel strongly that education has catapulted me into another sphere. In a sense, it's leveled the playing field and helped me to rise above my circumstances. I'm off to my next adventure and the next chapter in my career. My transformation has been inspired by mentors and family, but also my fierce determination to push forward and create my own reality. I hope I can leave a legacy of hope, grit, and determination for the next generation of young Latinas, to seek opportunity and start with education to get there.

REFLECT AND RISE

When faced with adversity, I invite you to consider these things:

Leave Your Legacy: Pay it forward and change will continue on through future generations.

Visualize Victory: Act "As If" you're there. It's always served me well.

Embrace the Bigger Picture: When you're forced to take a step back, you'll find you're able to leap forward in new ways you never thought possible.

BIOGRAPHY

As a second-generation Mexican American, Ariana Paz has built a career grounded in owning her bicultural, bilingual identity. She is a charismatic leader with over sixteen years of experience in human resources.

She's a driven change agent, prioritizing employee experience within established organizational workflows, and embraces her cultural duality as a key instrument in connecting to others. Currently in a strategic HR leadership role at CNA, Paz is guided by the desire to make an impact at a personal and organizational level, and leave a legacy of change in her wake. She connects with CEOs and senior leaders to frontline employees and influential movers and shakers to inspire organizational change.

Paz is the proud daughter of two self-made entrepreneurs and continues to stretch her own limits by pushing herself in realms where she can grow, and always seeks ways how she can give back to the Latino community. An International Business and Marketing graduate of University of Texas at San Antonio, she recently completed her MBA in Change Management from Kellstadt Graduate School of Business at DePaul University.

She's served as a mentor for young Latinas at Horizons for Youth and is an active member of Prospanica, Association of Latinos for America, and several other professional and cultural organizations supporting women and minorities in business.

Her lifetime goal is to be a positive role model, to inspire first- and second-generation Latinas who will forge paths of upward mobility and career advancement by breaking barriers in spaces that never seemed attainable and provide a sense of empowerment and belonging.

Ariana J. Paz
Director, Human Resources Business Partner
Years in HR: 16
Pazariana@gmail.com
Linkedin.com/in/arianapaz/

¡SÍ SE PUEDE!

KAYLA CASTRO KRUGER

"Embrace your past and forge your own future."

EL PRINCIPIO

I was born in Indio, California, to migrant farm workers that traveled up and down California following "la pisca" of different fruits and vegetables. While our parents were away for weeks at a time, my younger sister, Nayelly, and I lived in Mexicali, Baja California, with our Abuelita and our tiuchis (aunt). I was six years old when my papi decided it was time for us to move to the States with them so we could learn English and finally all live together. The move to Coachella, California, was a blur, but I do remember my first day of first grade, and the lasting and influential effect that my elementary school teachers had on me.

We lived in a trailer park on a ranch surrounded by fields filled with fruits and vegetables. The walk to our trailer from the bus stop felt like miles away for our little legs. One day, as I had just grown accustomed to our new routine, my mother was suddenly not there to pick us up. Holding Nayelly's hand, we walked with another parent back home, and when we arrived at our house, we were alone. A neighbor showed up sometime later and said we would stay with her. I vividly recall feeling lost and confused knowing my mom was not there. I have honestly never asked my father what happened that day, and after twenty-six years, I still cannot bring myself to ask what really led her to leave and never return. I was nine years old when I last saw her again. She was in a rehabilitation center in Mexicali, and she seemed fine. I remember she was happy to see us; however, I am not sure if I was happy to see her. I was just in limbo, confused as to who she really was and if it was even right to call her "Mami." I had so many questions, but I was so young, and not sure what to think or feel. I internalized those feelings, and moved on with my life until one fateful day many years later.

In June 2013, my husband and I decided to move to Seattle to pursue new professional opportunities. For months before that, I had considered reconnecting with my biological mother, but could not find the courage to do so. My mother was lost, and in order to find her, I would have to search the streets of Tijuana, Baja California. I was afraid, and did not know where to start. This professional opportunity was the perfect excuse to pause the search and hopefully gain the courage I needed to confront her in the future. While on the drive, nearing the beautiful Oregon coast, I had an epiphany. I came to the realization that I am courageous, and I did not need to find her for closure. Finally, after so many years, I could speak of my mother and begin to forgive her. All my memories of her before she left were beautiful. She was kind and caring and had the best impression of Kiko from *Chavo del Ocho!* I no longer wanted to be angry or blame her for leaving us. I physically felt the pain and anger leave my body. It was the most breathtaking feeling as the weight of so many years lifted off my shoulders. It was liberating, and I let go of so much resentment during that long drive. My heart started to heal, and I felt like I could start fresh and now pursue all my dreams.

A day after arriving in Seattle, my father and stepmother hesitantly called to let me know my mother had passed away from a drug-related infection. My father, a man who held his feelings strong, cried as he shared the unfortunate news. He was vulnerable, not to hard work or long hours in the fields, but for us, his children. I was not sure how to mourn her death. There were so many feelings, but none were anger. I was sad for her and her sudden death, and that I never told her I had forgiven her. Despite the hardships and struggles growing up,

I considered myself very fortunate. I had a very caring and present father, and a wonderful woman became my mother and created a safe and loving home for me. I also gained three more amazing siblings that I dearly love with all my heart.

LA ESCUELA

The first time I remember hearing about college was in third grade. Our teacher, Coach Reager, asked us to draw a picture of our future selves at our college graduation; we were the class of 2012! Since then, it seemed like that was the path I was destined for, and worked fearlessly toward that goal. I am not sure that Coach Reager will ever know just how much her classroom activity set me up for success. I am eternally grateful and will always cherish this activity as the moment my life took a turn for the best.

Through middle school and high school, I was in AVID, a college readiness program, and I was figuring out if I wanted to be a math teacher, elementary school teacher, or administrator. My dream was to return to the education system to create similar opportunities that were created for me. Not just in academics, but also because of all the emotional support I received from my teachers throughout the years. By the time I got to my senior year, I had finally chosen a career and the university I wanted to attend, Cal Poly Pomona. It was close enough to Coachella to visit home, but also far enough that it gave me independence. When I explained my decision to my father, he did not understand why I would want to go one hundred miles away to school. He was angry with me for wanting to leave, and I was crushed thinking I would have to defy my father to make my college dreams a reality. While I shared the crushing news with our Career Center team, Mrs. Alvarez, a spunky and chaparrita administrator, called my papi and convinced him to go on a campus visit. We picked a date, and Mrs. Alvarez drove us to visit my dream university. This beautiful, long-haired woman believed in my dream so much that she connected with my daddy about my future, and he listened. After visiting the university, my papi finally understood the importance and felt safe sending me to this new place. A few months later, when he drove me to college orientation, he made sure to tell me that he could pick me up and take me home at any time. I felt his sense of pride and fear. It was a new journey for us both, and we would need to learn how to be apart after all those years of being each other's support system.

MI CARRERA

My hospitality career started as a room attendant in 2008, and it has taken me to eight different hotels and three different states. I have been in human resources since 2015, and it has not been an easy journey. There were several failed interviews, lots of conversations about my future, and my own disbelief that this was a realistic goal. When I had finally earned my opportunity to enter HR, I still had to prove that I belonged. Becoming an HR professional began as an HR Coordinator, then HR Manager, then HR Coordinator again at an opening hotel, then Area Wellness Manager, and, currently, Area Recruiting Manager. As I gained confidence and understanding within HR, I wanted to be more than a professional. I also wanted to be a present mother and a loving and caring spouse. Being a brown, Spanish-speaking HR professional empowers me to continue learning and push away impostor syndrome, but I somehow continued to question my ability to parent and to support my wonderful husband. I have had to look deep into my dark brown eyes and see intelligence, resilience, and all the love I have to give. Not just because of all my father did to get me to where I am today, but I had to also give myself credit for all the work I put in to making sure his sacrifices were not in vain. Every time I think I might fail, I remember that my father did not cross a border and risk his life for a better future for us just so I could do the bare minimum. Finding a balance to honor my father and honoring my little family has been difficult. I want to do it all, and I have been amazing at times and have failed miserably at others.

The knowledge I have gained in human resources has helped me become a more confident person and has allowed me to genuinely help those in need. I have helped people dealing with life-changing events, and this has inspired me to keep learning so I may best support them. I am not afraid of asking questions and connecting with others to find an answer. I take new roles as a challenge and will fully immerse myself in them to become the "expert." With everything I am, I believe knowledge is power. Each day, I strive to be a little better. A better leader and professional, a better mami, and a better wife. I want to inspire others to believe in themselves, keep pushing forward, and never forget, "sí se puede."

REFLECT AND RISE

1. **Knowledge is power:** Whatever you want to learn, no one can take that away from you. Embrace your ability to absorb knowledge and sign up for all the free and paid webinars you can! Knowing a little bit of everything will help you find answers to all your questions.

2. **Be proud of where you came from and who you are:** Remember the sacrifices made by those around you and give credit where needed, but take credit for your achievements as well. We can be given the tools, but unless we do something with them, nothing will be accomplished.

3. **Care for others genuinely, and they will care for you too:** We are human, and genuine connections build trust. In our line of work, trust is necessary to thrive.

BIOGRAPHY

Kayla Irene Castro Kruger is a Mexican American Latina that resides in Southern California with her two beautiful children and amazingly guapo husband. She has a bachelor's in English Literature and a minor in Marketing from California Polytechnic University, Pomona. For most of her career she worked in hospitality and made her way into human resources in 2015. Kayla shares her story today to inspire and motivate others to never give up, be lifelong learners, and always have a "Sí Se Puede" attitude!

Kayla Castro Kruger
Area Recruiting Manager
Years in HR: 7
kicastro7@gmail.com
linkedin.com/in/castrokaylai/

EVERY DAY THE CLOCK RESETS

STEFANIE FURNISS

"I can't change the direction of the wind, but I can adjust my sails to always reach my destination."

I HAD MADE IT

It was 6:04 a.m. when I peeked at my phone. I didn't need an alarm anymore, but I always set it. I tiptoed out of bed and into the bathroom. I took the quickest shower, brushed my teeth, threw on the clothes, and got out of the house. It was 6:19 a.m. when I started my car. The ride to work was a decent commute, but it was a peaceful part of the morning and I still loved driving my new car. It was my needed alone time before walking into the daily organized chaos.

The clock read 7:02 a.m. when I pulled up into my parking spot at the University Faculty Club. The parking lot led into the nicest, smallest, and most exclusive venue on campus. My career had been evolving and progressing quickly, but recently it felt like I had blinked and four years at the university had gone by. I was now completing my second year as Director of Operations for the food contract group.

Prior to this, and for almost fifteen years, I was in food and beverage management for restaurant chains. While I was no stranger to working ridiculously long hours, this shift into the contract industry now felt different. The contract industry had new layers to it. It was more refined, it came with perks, with weekends off, with parking spots, and better hours. It made the responsibility of managing nineteen units consisting of 220+ associates a lot more bearable, even fun.

TIME KEEPS TICKING

7:08 a.m. when I looked at the clock again. Time to get started. My office now was very different from the old offices earlier in my career that used to be in tiny storage rooms. I walked in and saw the boxes of marketing memorabilia sitting on my couch.

I should clean this up right now. No, wait. First, I need coffee, I thought to myself.

I turned the corner that led to the Starbucks when I almost bumped into Silvana.

"Is it seven o'clock already? *Café? Te lo traigo.* I don't have the blonde roast until the truck comes, but we just brewed Pikes."

I'm not sure when it happened, but a while back, she started bringing me coffee to my office in the morning. I never really knew whether she did it as an act of kindness, a smart move to keep me out of the Starbucks store, or just to chat for a bit before she went back to the grind. Literally. Regardless of the reason, I loved it, and she always said something random and funny that snapped me to the present.

"I love what you've done with the place," she said as she handed me a coffee. "You could at least refill the Skittles."

I stared at the pictures I had in my office. I hadn't gotten around to elaborate decorating, but the few photos of my family always made me smile. At the top corner of my wall was Valeria, my baby niece. It was her first school picture. She was almost eight months old, but she still had little rolls on her arms that always made me want to squish her.

"Are you gonna get that?" Silvana asked. "The phone." She pointed at it.

The day flew by. It was 5:52 p.m. before I noticed. I had meant to leave earlier today, but as I was heading back to my office, my phone rang. The pipe burst at the medical campus and I had to wait until it was repaired to make sure we could open tomorrow. It was 6:24 p.m. when Jesse popped in.

"Thanks for taking care of that. Want to catch the last drink at happy hour? My treat."

Happy hour? Now? Could I finally bring it up? I wasn't sure I was ready to talk to him, but I looked up at him smiling and nodded.

"Yeah, sure. Why not?"

Anxiety snuck up on me as I realized I was going to talk to Jesse. Most times I looked forward to having a glass of wine with him where I'd share the crazy stories of the week and he'd sneak in advice, but today was different. I had to talk to him. I had to tell him how I felt. Ultimately, no matter what happened today, I had to resign. Would I do it?

FROM DREAM JOB TO A NEW DREAM

Three months before tonight's happy hour, I had gone for my annual checkup with Dr. Raymin. I loved her. She was great and so straightforward, and real, but this time she left me stumped.

"Need another script for birth control?" she asked.

"No, doc, we're not using that anymore, remember? Whatever happens, happens," I joked.

"Oh, yeah, that's right. Wait, has nothing happened yet? Weren't you off birth control last year?"

"Yeah. It's taking a little bit longer than we thought, but we'll just give it some good old practice," I joked.

"So, when did you start trying?" she asked.

"Well, really trying, over a year ago, I guess."

"You've been off the pill for a year?"

"No, a while before that."

"If you've been off birth control for more than two years, then you've been trying for that long. It may be time to explore options. Would you consider seeing a specialist?"

I remember feeling a pit in my stomach. I hadn't realized how long it had been. Every month, like clockwork, another period, then another event, then another victory team lunch, or open house party, and then I'd blink and a month would pass and the loop began again.

I searched for the first appointment with the fertility clinic. Since my first visit, and to this present day happy hour, I had been seen eighteen times. I had blood work, tests, checkups, and even the first of many procedures. After lots of research, a bunch of needles, and a bit of tears, the summary of my medical chart was that I had diminished ovarian reserve. I was actually running out of chances, out of time.

The past ninety days had been a whirlwind of stress, and a balancing act of responsibilities that included shifting appointments, getting to work late somedays, and leaving early others. A new silent panic had set in. I was tired and I felt guilty. Jesse had been accommodating my requests, but how much longer could I keep this up?

HAPPY HOUR?

"You better eat some of this bacon that you made me order for your Keto shmeto diet," said Jesse. "Otherwise, I would've ordered the calamari."

Jesse often fronted being bossy, but could always point out a detail that could improve a project, a person, or even a team. This was how he masked his empathy and balanced his unyielding loyalty.

I reached for the bacon…

"I need to take some time for myself. I need to take a break. I think I need to change what I'm doing daily," I told Jesse.

"OK, take a few days if that's what you need," he said.

"I think I need to take a lot more than that," I almost whispered to him.

"Like how much? This almost sounds like you're quitting, Stef."

We sat there awkwardly for a few minutes. Neither of us said anything for longer than a minute. I finally broke the silence.

"I think I am."

I mustered the courage to look him in the eye. I was nervous, more than I had anticipated, because today I wasn't just talking to my boss, I was also telling my friend. Another long pause as he cupped his drink.

"But this is Hotel California," he said. "You can check out any time you like, but you can never leave."

We laughed. Then we paused. Then we nervously laughed some more.

IF YOU BUILD IT, IT WILL COME

I had done it. I had said it. I had played this moment in my head over and over in the last couple of weeks, because I knew I now wanted more. Alongside my professional success, I wanted to take a moment to grow my personal life too. I had spent decades building my work persona, but very little time nurturing my personal goals.

After months of debating whether I "should" leave a good career, I ran up to the metaphorical red emergency button of life and slammed it hard. Pause; time out, time to reevaluate. As soon as the words "I think I need a lot more than that" came out of my mouth, everything changed.

And it worked. And I got more.

Funny enough, Jesse ended up being right; he almost always is. I resigned my role as Director of Operations, but I never left "Hotel California." After verbalizing a desire to change professional gears, new paths presented themselves and I found myself working in HR. It was not always easy, nor was it just a miraculous manifestation into a new career. But it had been the definitive moment when I had the courage to do what I *wanted* that led to my life shift and current career. I had the conviction to move differently because I was looking for a different result. After years of depositing into my career, I got to this moment of peak strength where I could make a withdrawal and invest in myself.

REFLECT AND RISE

- *"Todo con moderación."* I've heard this phrase since I was a tiny little girl. My mother has been repeating this to me since I could remember. It's my verbal reminder to find balance. She must have known I was more prone to extremes; all or nothing.

    - Is there a portion or aspect of your life that you'd like to spend more time on? Is there something you want to do less, differently, or better?

- It's been said that the definition of insanity is repeating the same thing over and over but seeking different results. I challenge you:

- Who is the last person you met that was very different from you? How did you manage these differences? What can you learn from this person?
- When was the last time you tried something new and challenged yourself? When did you last step out of your routine?

- *"Querer es poder."* The biggest projects and most lavish successes start with an idea.
  - What little voice in your head has been getting louder and louder? Are you letting that little voice speak, and are you willing to listen?
  - If you haven't verbalized or visualized your goal, take an hour this week to spend on meditation, walking, or yoga. At the start of your hour, set an intention for that moment.

BIOGRAPHY

Stefanie Furniss was born and raised in Miami, Florida. She is a first-generation Americana to a Colombian mom and Costa Rican dad that moved as newlyweds to the States for new opportunities. Never shy to work (or anything, really), she started working in food and beverage to make ends meet while attending Florida State University. She now has over twenty years of experience in building great teams that produce successful results.

In 2003, her career started in restaurant management and quickly advanced as she leaned into her passion for training and people development. In the past five years, Stefanie crossed over from operations to human resources after spending a year consulting and developing new business for her previous employer. Currently, she is a Talent Acquisition Manager for Marc Lore's new start-up venture, *Wonder*, based out of New Jersey.

While she has enjoyed a couple of decades in the hospitality industry, her favorite "job" is her most recent promotion to Mamá. Her star employees are a two-year-old daughter named Laura, often called "mini CEO," and Laura's younger sister, Lucia, the "Chief People Officer." In her journey to this recent stage in her life, she's rerouted her priorities to finally follow her own mother's advice to always seek balance, "todo con moderación." Though she's only a yogi in her own mind, Stefanie now recharges regularly through movement, a good game night, or finally getting a full night's rest. This helps her keep an infectious energy in both work and play.

>Stefanie Furniss
>Talent Acquisition Manager
>Years in HR: 5
>Linkedin.com/in/stefanie-furniss-8a04a297/
>Instagram: @Stef2944

IT'S NEVER TOO LATE TO ACHIEVE YOUR DREAMS

MONICA CRISTAL GAONA

"It's your life. YOU are responsible for your results. Risk, Attempt, Fail, and Succeed."

TIME FOR A CHANGE

It was 2:33 a.m. and I couldn't sleep again. I was dreading another day at my job. I didn't want to be there another day, but what could I do? I had no backup plan. I had three little ones that depended on my paycheck to survive. My job had become routine for me where I was bored, uninspired, while struggling living paycheck to paycheck. My parents didn't understand when I told them how unhappy I was at work. *"¿Ay, mija, para qué quieres irte a otro trabajo? Allí te ayudan con la aseguranza y son flexibles con las horas del trabajo por los niños."*

My job covered my insurance and had a flexible schedule, but it wasn't my passion or what I wanted to do for the rest of my life. My parents came from Mexico at a young age. Success for them did not have the same meaning for me. Their definition of success was job security and stability. For many years I had put my dream on hold. As a mother of three children, I wanted to be there for every milestone but also not neglect my aspirations. No one understood what I felt that morning. I was determined to put Monica first and fight to make her dreams come true. I knew one way or another, I was not going to let little Monica down—the one who had dreams to do big things in life. Today was the day I made the change.

FAMILY EXPECTATIONS

In 2008, I graduated with my bachelor's degree in Public Administration from Cal State University Dominguez Hills. I was the first person in my family to graduate from college. It was a huge accomplishment for me and my family, as I wanted to be the best role model for my siblings.

Working as an account payable clerk for five years, I was constantly asked, "What are you doing with your degree?" I felt embarrassed saying the truth: I didn't know.

When I got married at twenty-two years old, I thought love was everything, but it wasn't. When my second daughter was born in 2011, my husband had to leave the country to obtain his green card. I was left all alone with two little ones. I struggled financially, emotionally, and mentally. In order to make ends meet, I asked for government assistance and was denied. How could I not qualify? All my money went to cover rent and bills. How was I going to feed my girls? Our financial problems on top of being separated were starting to affect my marriage. Desperate, I asked my boss if I could assist in special projects to get more money. He agreed.

When I thought of HR, I thought it was just about hiring and firing employees. Ninety percent of the employees at the downtown Los Angeles produce market were Spanish speakers and always had questions regarding labor laws. *"Señora, tengo preguntas de la aseguransa."* Well, I wasn't in charge of benefits; however, I felt the need to assist. As years went by, employees saw me as the go-to person for work issues. It started with just answering their questions, and before I knew it, I was doing employee relations, recruitment, and benefits.

For the next five years, my passion grew as I continued doing accounting and HR. Ten years after I obtained my bachelor's degree, I started researching schools that had master's programs in HR. I registered in 2018, not knowing if I was going to get accepted. When I told my family that I had applied for the master's program at Azusa Pacific

University, I was surprised by their reactions. *"Ya tienes un buen trabajo y los niños. ¿Cómo lo vas a hacer?"* These were not the reactions I wanted to hear, but I wasn't going to allow their comments to change my mind. Despite not receiving the support I was hoping for from my family and going back to school later in life, I was determined to pursue my dreams for myself.

THE HR STRUGGLES

"Happy Thursday! It is with great pleasure that we select you for admission into the Master's of Business Management with Human Resource Management program for the Fall 2018 Term!"

I got in. I couldn't believe it. I was nervous, excited, while crying, full of mixed emotions. I was a mom of three starting a master's program and working full time. *¿Cómo le iba a hacer?* How was I going to do it? I didn't know how, but I was determined to make my dreams happen.

One year into the master's program, I was ready to move on from my comfort zone, or at least I thought I was ready. I felt prepared to put into play what I learned from my past experiences and what I was learning while in school.

After being with the same company for more than ten years, I put myself back in the job market. I opened my first account on Indeed.com and began my search for my first HR Manager role. One month went by and I did not hear back. What was I doing wrong? My sister reviewed my resume and she suggested if I was going into the HR field, to omit my accounting work history and only focus on the HR experience. But even after changing my resume, the next three months were full of countless rejection emails. It was a heart-breaking moment for me. I felt defeated. I wanted to know what I was doing wrong. I asked recruiters for feedback and they all had the same thing to say, I did not have leadership experience and I should consider only HR Generalist roles. HR Generalist was what I was already doing. Why would I continue doing the same job? I was upset, angry, and frustrated. I threw away my resume and started all over. I practiced my interviewing skills with my cousin and sister. I was not going to give up on the manager role that I knew was waiting for me.

THE OPPORTUNITY

After one particular rejection email, I got a call from a VP of HR for a job I had applied for as HR Director asking if I would be interested in another position as an HR Manager for a separate division in the city of El Monte. I met with the president of the organization. She was very welcoming, and I felt an instant connection. The organization services and manages housing for low-income families, seniors, as well as the chronic mentally ill. One week later, I received an offer.

My first task as an HR Manager was not an easy one. Within a month in my new position, we experienced the first global pandemic. Navigating through the unknown and learning a new industry was a challenge. That same year, the company decided to initiate a new electronic HRIS system.

Every day was a learning experience. Most days I felt overwhelmed as I worked many late nights. For months I cried at night, feeling exhausted, uncertain, doubting myself if I had done the right move in seeking a manager position. Was I ready to be a manager? Maybe it was too soon and I needed more experience. I quickly snapped out of those thoughts. Failing was not an option for me. I was not going to disappoint my children. I was determined to not to give up and to prove that the challenges were not going to stop me from successfully doing my job.

HARD WORK PAYS OFF

In just four months, I successfully trained management and hourly staff in the new HRIS system. During the second year with the organization, they announced they were going to merge with another company. Changes were about to occur. The Affordable Housing Division was going to expand to add nine more communities to the Northern California region.

It was Friday afternoon on my way home from work

when I received a call from the company president. I remember her saying, "Monica, we are going to be promoting you to HR Director. You have done an outstanding job, and the VP of HR and myself know you are ready for the promotion." I was in shock as tears of joy flooded my eyes. I am still so grateful to the president of the company for supporting and giving me the opportunity that I worked so hard to accomplish.

Gracias virgencita.

Ever since I started my career transition, I would turn on my candle to Lady of Guadalupe. Growing up in a Catholic household, I always held my beliefs and my faith to Our Lady of Guadalupe. During the interview process, I prayed to her to guide me to a job where I can be happy, make a difference, and achieve my career goals. I believe she made things happen for me at the right place at the right time. All those rejection emails happened because I was meant to be here. It was a sign from her leading me to where I am today. With her guidance and a lot of hard work, I will continue to strive toward my ultimate career goal in becoming a VP in HR.

REFLECT AND RISE

Many ask me, why human resources?

For me, it was the desire to help others and have a positive impact in an organization. Many will have their reasons. There will be plenty of highs and lows along the way. Here's some advice for someone who is starting in an HR career.

- Don't be afraid to start over: It may take up to ten years to get a new degree or specific certifications. There will be times when you will feel like you can't do it; however, don't get discouraged. It can take time to find the position of your dreams, but keep going until you land the right one.

- Work from your heart: That comes into play when you do the human part in Human resources. Do what you feel is right. To be successful, you will need to have a strong sense of ethics, honesty, and integrity. Smile because smiling helps employees feel at ease and creates a positive environment and better company culture.

- Speak up: I didn't wait for the leadership team to ask for my opinions. When I saw an opportunity to improve the work structure, I would bring my recommendations and ideas to management, whether it was training managers on a strategy or providing payroll training for staff. Some ideas were welcomed, some were not; however, your voice defines the value you bring to the organization.

BIOGRAPHY

Monica Cristal Gaona is currently an HR Director for a nonprofit organization. She manages the HR department for the Affordable Housing division. In her role, she oversees employee relations, benefits, payroll, leave administration, and performance management. She discovered her passion in HR while helping and coaching employees. Monica started working in small to midsize companies and has successfully helped transition and implement HRIS systems.

Monica is Mexican/American and was raised in Pico Rivera, California. She holds a bachelor's degree in Public Administration with a concentration in Administration Managements from California State University Dominguez Hills and a master's in Business Management with an emphasis in Human Resources from Azusa Pacific University.

Monica is a proud mother of two girls and one boy. She enjoys traveling and being a team mom for her children's soccer teams. She is grateful for her husband of fifteen years that has given her the support in her career's goals.

Monica Cristal Gaona
HR Director
Years in HR: 10
Monicagaona325@gmail.com
Linkedin.com/in/gaonam

BREAKING INTO HR, THE NONTRADITIONAL WAY

ANGÉLICA PATLÁN

"Always believe that the impossible is possible."
—Selena Quintanilla-Perez

"You don't have a dad. Who are you going to make a card for?"

I remember the moment a grade-school classmate asked me this while making Father's Day cards. They were right, I did not have a father. I was the daughter of a single mother who had me when she was nineteen. It was at this moment, as my cheeks felt hot and flushed with color as time seemed to slow down, that I first knew what it meant to be different. From that moment on, I did everything I could to never feel that way again.

Growing up in San Jose, California, my mom, maternal grandparents, and maternal uncle instilled in me the importance of education and its ability to take me wherever I wanted to go in life. From a young age, my mom put me in private schools where my love of learning took off. In the seventh grade, when it was clear my current school was not a good environment, she marched into the principal's office of a small private school thirty minutes from our home and managed to get me in on financial aid. I still remember the drive there on my first day of school. The lump in my throat grew the closer we got, and when I arrived, it felt like my stomach had dropped to my toes. I was the new girl and one of four non-white students in my class. It was the first time I had experienced being in a predominantly white environment, and I quickly had to learn how to adapt. I sensed that familiar feeling of being different lurking as I was the only person with one parent, did not live in the wealthy surrounding suburbs, and initially struggled due to the advanced curriculum. But after pouring myself into my studies, I found that I was able to keep pace with my classmates and take part in conversations that I hadn't had before. We talked about how to be accepted into a good college and what it meant to be successful in life. It was during these conversations that I began formulating a plan to not only become successful, but to never feel different again.

STEP 1: GET INTO A GREAT HIGH SCHOOL AND GRADUATE.

After successfully navigating my way through my last two years of middle school, I attended an all-girls private high school in San Jose. I was no longer one of four non-white students and found myself surrounded by diverse girls and people who empowered me to seek more for myself. This support was vital when I found out that the odds were not in my favor as the daughter of a single mother. I remember sitting at a computer in the school's library and staring at the computer screen that held the words: "Daughters of teen mothers are three times more likely to become teen mothers themselves and less likely to finish high school." My stomach was in knots. I began to feel a fire ignite inside my soul. That was not going to be me.

During my four years of high school, I played sports, participated in clubs, took AP classes, and at the end I was accepted to a liberal arts college in Northampton, Massachusetts. I had done it! I had beaten the statistics and was that much closer to my goal.

STEP 2: GO TO A GOOD COLLEGE AND GET A DEGREE.

In August of 2010, I stepped onto Smith College's campus as a freshman. Surrounded by brick buildings and beautiful New England nature, I was overwhelmed by the feeling of opportunity and I felt like success was at my fingertips.

Yet, I can't lie, those four years were some of the toughest in my life and tested not only my resolve, but my ability to stick to my plans. It became clear that while I had excelled in high school, the courses at Smith were exponentially tougher. I remember sitting in my lecture hall and hearing but not understanding what my professor was saying. I looked around at my classmates and thought, *What am I doing here? I don't belong here.* The feeling of being different emerged from hiding and was exacerbated by the fact that, as a Latina, I was a part of a small minority on campus. Soon, I began to question myself, my abilities, and whether I could really hack it at this college. It wasn't until I found my place in Anthropology and Residence Life that I decided to stay.

After a tough freshman year, I had managed to improve academically, and in May of 2014 I graduated with a BA in Anthropology and a minor in Exercise Science. Then came the question, "Now what?"

STEP 3: GET A GOOD JOB AND BE SUCCESSFUL.

After graduation, I returned home to California without a clue of what was next. By happenstance, I applied and was accepted to train as a 911 radio dispatcher for a local police department. I finally felt like I had made it; I had the degree and a good-paying job. Yet, not long after I started, I began to see signs that this good job with good pay came at a price.

The first sign occurred when I was training as a call taker and having a hard time getting information from a caller. The radio dispatcher working my call stood up from across the room and screamed at me in front of the entire control room. I had never experienced anything like that before, and I remember my trainer coming to me saying, "Oh, that's just how they are." The next sign came when a supervisor pulled me into their office and told me that I needed to wear my uniform when I walked into work because "I had a nice body and people wouldn't like me." I walked out of that office feeling self-conscious and confused. I felt myself shrinking within the walls of the workplace, trying to make myself as small as possible. There were many signs after that, and with each one, I felt my voice, my passion, and my sense of self dwindling. But I had worked too hard to get this far to quit, and so I did what my family taught me: I put my head down and worked hard. I signed up for excessive amounts of overtime and worked high-profile events so that they could see my value as an employee. But with each overtime shift and the more hours I spent in this environment, I began to feel the heaviness of burnout, the crushing weight of anxiety, and a gnawing feeling that I was not where I should be. Almost four years later, I woke up one morning and stood at my bathroom sink. As I looked in the mirror, I did not recognize who was staring back at me. Her face was dull and her eyes were lifeless and full of pain. It took me several moments to realize that the woman

I was looking at was me. My mind could only piece together a single question, "How did I get here?" I had followed the plan for success: I had beat the odds, graduated high school and college, and landed a good job. This wasn't supposed to happen.

CHANGE OF PLANS

It took me months to detach myself from the dispatcher identity I had clung to, and as I reflected on my last four years, the same question kept coming up, "Who was supposed to be there for me as an employee?" The answer I kept coming back to was HR. After researching the field, I decided to pursue a master's degree in Human Resource Management and graduated in 2020. Similar to my early years, I thought if I had the degree, then opportunities would open up for me, so I was surprised when I was met with a brick wall. Every position I applied to responded with, "I don't see how your past experience is HR related" or "You don't have enough experience." So I tried to mold myself into what I thought the industry wanted. I figured if I could hide my differences, I could make it. But nothing changed, and it came to a point where I knew that I would have to do something radical if I wanted to break into the industry. I would have to stop running from my differences and embrace my nontraditional journey.

In July of 2020, I started posting on LinkedIn about my past work experiences and how those led me to the field of HR. I can remember the initial thought of "Why would what I have to say matter?" but I pushed through the initial fear and doubt. I had something to say and I was not hiding anymore. By doing so, I was able to meet so many wonderful HR professionals who shared the same passion as me to make the world of work a better place. One of these professionals invited me on her podcast, and when an HR Generalist position opened up at her company in May of 2021, she became my supervisor. Now a little less than a year and a half later, I have two positions under my belt and I am now a People Operations Partner for a remote tech company. As I think back to that little girl who wished she could be anything but different and to the woman who felt like her nontraditional background would never land her an HR job, I would tell them this: our world needs different and nontraditional, so own your story and trust the journey. You are worthy of everything your heart desires. Go after it.

REFLECT AND RISE

When you're thinking about a career in HR but you've never held an HR job before, the path before you can seem daunting, and at times, insurmountable. Even more so if you have a nontraditional background or have been a part of a hostile work environment. I see you and want to share some advice with you.

1. Lean into the uncomfortable feelings. When you are making a change as big as this, it can feel overwhelmingly uncomfortable, and there may be a part of you that wants to return to what feels familiar. Don't. Comfort keeps you stagnant and in the same cycle.

2. Remember your why. The path is not always linear or easy. In fact, it can be downright hard and demotivating, which makes it imperative that you remember why you want to go into HR. What sparked your interest? What lights you up about this path? Hold those answers in your mind during dark times and use them as fuel.

3. Don't sell yourself or your experience short. Sure, you may not have traditional HR experience, but your experience still matters. In your journey, you may run into people who encourage you to settle or take positions that do not honor your experience and your worth. Be strategic about your next move (if you're financially able to, of course): ensure the company deserves you, make sure your manager is someone you want to work with, and that this position aligns with your career goals.

4. Remember you are worthy, valuable, and needed. You can get into HR and practice HR the nontraditional way.

BIOGRAPHY

Angélica Patlán was born and raised in the Bay Area and attended Smith College in Massachusetts. She has a background in Anthropology and graduated with a Master of Science in Human Resource Management from SNHU. Angélica is dedicated to putting the human in the title back into the forefront of the human resources space and organizations as a whole. Her passion and dedication derive from her own experiences in the workplace. These experiences guided her to her true calling, which is to champion and advocate for employees with the ultimate goal of humanizing the work experience. She is currently the People Operations Partner at JustAnswer, where she focuses on onboarding and the employee experience. Outside of work, she can be found drinking coffee, lifting weights, reading books, and being out in beautiful Bay Area nature.

Angélica Patlán
People Operations Parter
Years in HR: 2
angelica.o.patlan@gmail.com
Linkedin.com/in/apatlan/

FAILING FORWARD: LEANING INTO OUR STRENGTHS AND GROWTH

ARELY LAGUNAS

"The Past is your Lesson. The Present is your Gift. The Future is your Motivation."
—Zig Ziglar

I am not a teacher by profession, but within the field of HR, education is a key component, and I have a profound appreciation for it. I was a third-grader when this passion was ignited by the encouraging and bright Mrs. Johnson. She brought out the best in her students by challenging us to master new skills. She had such a positive influence on me that I began to explore the idea of becoming an educator. I wanted to make a lasting impact just like Mrs. Johnson had on me. I am grateful to be able to combine my love for education and knowledge to what I do today.

This year I celebrated fifteen years in the field of human resources and twenty-one years of entering the workforce. In 2019, I took a leap of faith to continue to build HR Consulting and focus on my strengths to fuel my creativity muscle. I am grateful to partner with different industries and small businesses, primarily in the Hispanic community, to support HR initiatives while cultivating a work-life integration, and be more present at home with my family. The best part is that through this journey, I dedicated time to lean into my calling and found immense fulfillment serving as a Career and Leadership coach.

We've all heard the saying "Knowledge is power." My goal has been to increase my knowledge to apply it to my personal and professional journey. As an HR Practitioner, I strive to educate employees, influence positive behaviors, and embrace a high-performance culture to align to the company's mission and objectives. As a coach, I am committed to empowering individuals with tools to navigate and support their career. It's not just finding the right people but also providing the tools, resources, and culture to help employees succeed in their work environment.

ADVOCATING FOR YOURSELF

I learned about the power of advocacy and coaching through my career in HR while empowering employees on their rights and responsibilities. This was something I recognized early on as a need and of high importance in our communities. Many laws today, unfortunately, did not exist fifty years ago. My mother was terminated from her job in 1988 for taking frequent breaks to the bathroom due to her pregnancy complications. She had hyperemesis gravidarum (excessive nausea and vomiting). Coincidentally, I also had HG with my firstborn son that lasted seven months of my pregnancy. The outcome of our stories was different. I had a supportive manager, and I understood employee rights due to my education as an HR professional. The Pregnancy Discrimination Act passed in 1978 prohibited discrimination against employees based on pregnancy, childbirth, or pregnancy-related medication conditions.

Prior to the Act, there were various Supreme Court cases that dealt with issues of employment discrimination against pregnant women and demonstrated a need for protections from this type of discrimination (Jurist.org).

Unfortunately, like many of our immigrant parents who came to a new country to seek a better life, learning and adapting to a new country takes time. I am glad my mother's friend advised her what the employer had done was illegal and to seek further guidance. My mother followed her friend's advice and asked to return to work in addition to back pay granted during the time she was terminated.

Stories like this remind me of the critical importance of educating employers on employment laws and practicing empathy toward employees. Using our powerful voices to boldly and diplomatically speak up about topics and concerns that matter to us is essential. It has been my mission to provide resources to employees by being an advocate in HR and providing guidance to employers on compliance. Quite frankly, employees take care of their employer when employers genuinely take care of their employees. It is a win-win situation when both are aligned.

FOCUSING ON THE LESSON TO CONTINUE TO GROW

I found valuable lessons early on in my journey as a first-generation professional Latina and mother in Corporate America.

In 2015, at thirty years old, I was working for a company and my career path was flourishing. I was also working for the second time with one of the best managers and most genuine leaders in HR I have ever met. As the company grew and was acquired by a global company, I began to report to a new manager. I witnessed firsthand how this manager belittled other colleagues on a consistent basis and expressed microaggressions. In particular, this leader expressed that my FMLA leave was "vacation time." Upon my return from FMLA with my second child, he expected me to log on remotely as early as 5 a.m. to attend a global meeting that was not required for my role. I left my job when I was seven months pregnant with my third child. I did not have a solid plan. I only knew I did not want to continue to be in that environment. I learned how powerful it feels to walk away from situations that do not serve me. I prioritize my emotional and mental well-being because I wanted that for my unborn son. I wanted to focus on my pregnancy and our health.

This decision was one of the hardest decisions I have made in my life because I knew it would impact not just me but also my husband and soon-to-be-three children. Though it was challenging, I do not regret it. It left me with so many valuable life lessons I still apply today. My backup plan was to build an HR consultancy clientele in order to be present at home with my family while contributing to the workforce. I knew it would require time, patience, dedication, and resources to build clientele, and it would not happen overnight. I learned quickly it would also require climbing the hardest mountain to see the best views. Often I heard that designing a life around motherhood that gives fulfillment and freedom without sacrificing our well-being was looking for a unicorn. I wanted to dismantle this narrative and show others they can do it too.

Adding a growing family from three members to five members in one year, managing an emotional rollercoaster of pregnancy hormones, mitigating financial changes, while grieving the unexpected loss of my grandma was not a walk in the park. In fact, I felt lost at one point and felt physically and mentally exhausted. I was able to reconnect with myself after two challenging years of rebuilding back up all aspects of my life. I learned tremendously about my relationship with money and financial literacy. I made many adjustments and changes that were necessary to ensure we could continue to afford our house and provide the necessities for our growing family. I learned to honor my physical, mental, and emotional well-being by acknowledging it and obtaining help, something I really never had done before.

ACTIVATING A GROWTH MINDSET

At thirty years old, during one of the most pivotal moments of my life, I asked myself, "Am I purposefully living my life? What is stopping me from achieving my full potential?" The answer was self-imposed limitations, fear, and a lack of confidence. It all started with activating a growth mindset. I began to concentrate on my strengths rather than my weaknesses to help boost my confidence. I accepted challenging opportunities leading me outside of my comfort zone. I learned to trust myself and I began to set healthy boundaries in all areas of my life. I continue to work daily on my growth mindset.

Prioritizing inner peace and leaning into my strengths is due to the inner work and growth mindset I have been intentionally developing and executing consistently in the last three years. Because life is full of sprinkles of highs and lows, I have started to do monthly check-ins of my wins. No matter how big or small, it is important to acknowledge those wins. Particularly in our Latino community, where wins are often not amplified or are seen as immodest. Creating space to toot your own horn before you can do the same to others. Wins will be a reminder of your progress when things go south or when you need an extra motivational push.

TRUSTING THE PROCESS

I have a deep regard for reading and writing. Becoming an author has sparked a new interest and desire. I learned to journal in sixth grade and last year I began to journal again. Suddenly the stars aligned and routed me to this wonderful community of Latinas in HR.

It has been a winding journey full of concealed lessons that allowed me to redefine my core values and priorities. From early in my career, I experienced a position elimination in 2008 during the recession to accepting pay cuts while searching for work-life integration. I knew this was not the only approach. I was eager to find a new way that allowed me to earn what I have worked hard for and be present at home with my family. I appreciate these seasons of flying high and low because it allows me to practice days of gratitude and days of prayer. Using my voice, advocating for myself, and honoring my own potential allowed me to bounce back from any roadblocks along the way and transcend beyond those limitations. I found these lessons very valuable to amplify our voices where historically Latinas and women of color have been underrepresented in leadership roles. The gap is even greater for mothers in the workplace. As an immigrant to a new country, finding representation and community was essential to my growth and confidence. I am honored to be part of the movement in Latina empowerment and cultivating spaces for representation.

I continue to evolve and commit to the process. Learning to live in the present has forced me to rest and reflect. My goal is to create an abundant mindset around me and hopefully in others. Through my leadership roles in HR, my purpose is to create a teachable environment for individuals to lead—an experience I learned early on in third grade with Mrs. Johnson. We need more leaders who inspire and motivate while adding value to others (John C Maxwell). I am a firm believer that leadership is not born but made. We can all embark on becoming a leader from where we are regardless of experience, background, or walk of life.

REFLECT AND RISE

Don't be afraid of failing forward. It's part of your own journey to success.

Never stop believing in yourself and what you are capable of accomplishing.

Protect your dreams and aspirations.

Be your own advocate and celebrate your voice.

Live a fulfilling and purposeful journey.

BIOGRAPHY

Arely Lagunas is a first-generation Latina. She was born in Mexico and raised in the United States. Arely is a mother of three children and has been married to her husband for thirteen years. She is also a Human Resources Practitioner with fifteen years of experience collaborating with businesses in various industries ranging from nonprofit, manufacturing, trucking, automotive, restaurant, and catering. Driven by her first-gen experience navigating new territories and Arely's passion for education inspired her to launch Creative Achievers Network (CAN!) in 2018, empowering youth and millennials in career building, leadership, and financial literacy tools.

More recently, Arely launched Dropping Gems Con Muchos Colores Podcast in September of 2021 to celebrate Latina motherhood voices leading with purpose, breaking barriers, and chasing bold dreams. Arely is also a board member of Latinas on the Plaza, a nonprofit organization to help women of color rise to their full potential. Arely graduated from DePaul University with a Bachelor of Science degree in Management. Arely also holds a Master of Science degree in Human Resource Management from Capella University.

Arely Lagunas

HR Consultant

Years in HR: 15

arelylagunasmtz@gmail.com

Facebook: Creative Achievers Network (Career & Leadership Coaching)

Facebook: Dropping Gems Con Muchos Colores Podcast

Instagram: @creativeachieversnetworkcan

Instagram: @droppinggemsconmuchoscolorespodcast

AM I THE ONLY ONE IN THE ROOM OR AM I JUST DREAMING?

CAROLINA M. VEIRA

"Inside of us, we have all the tools we need to accomplish all we want and be successful. We just need to focus on what we are good at and take action. The universe will take care of the rest. Dream bigger, be patient, and believe in yourself, deeply and shamelessly."

I ask myself this question as I sip my morning coffee during my mental quest to try to solve the problems of the world—or my little world, for that matter.

I am a dreamer, but one of those dreamers who dream big and take action. I am all about action, always moving, no matter how big or small the steps, even if that means moving backward to then move forward. I just have to keep moving and doing. When I get stuck, I die. But that road has not necessarily been the most crowded. It can get lonely. At times, one can be surrounded by people who are aligned with you. And then, solitude.

It is all part of the process.

I remember being in my early twenties, working for a private equity firm that invested in renewable energy. I oversaw all the administrative functions dealing with everything from HR to Marketing and Communications for a power plant in Upstate New York. Here's where my love for all things Buffalo Bills was born. But I digress. I was introduced to sustainability concepts when only California believed it was possible to live sustainably and make a profit at the same time. I got exposed to some of the brightest minds, who were also all white male and in their mid-thirties and mid-forties. You can imagine how challenging that period was for this Latina soul sister. I was learning about sustainability, investing, project management, and business development from top executives while supporting a group of ex-Navy folks who were also all white males. I was not only the only female employee, but I was young, not as experienced as them, but very scrappy and perseverant. Very stubborn and proudly Latina.

Yep, those were the times.

I had to prove myself every step of the way. With the Navy folks, I had to ensure they knew that I was cool, but not interested in sleeping with them, because, trust me, that was what they always thought. Somehow, asking about their weekend translated into *Let's kiss and see where this goes next.*

And then there were the California folks. I was so determined to make them like me that I was blinded at times by my desire for them to see me a certain way. I just had to be me. Cliché, I know, but sometimes the simplest answer is the best answer, and we don't necessarily see it.

I will never forget Dan Seif. He was a mentor to me without him ever knowing he would be such an important person in my life. You never know how your words can impact someone else. This is true about him. At some point he was in charge of the asset, and I had the chance to work with him on one of the simplest and most important projects of my life. And so, I researched some items he requested, I organized, summarized, and made it look pretty. I presented the info to Dan and he looked surprised. I don't know if his expectations of what I could do were very low, or maybe the project was harder than what I thought and I did not see it. Who knows? He then proceeded to *regalarme* one of the most memorable moments of my life.

Dan: This is really great work, Carolina!

Carolina: (Confused but happy) Thank you, Dan.

Dan: Carolina, why don't you risk it all and just go for it?

Carolina: It?

Dan: Go for an Ivy League education.

Carolina: (More confused than ever in my life. Thinking – do you even know how expensive that is? Well, yes, you know, because you attended an Ivy League) Me? No!

Let me make a parenthesis here. When you are born Latina, you have parents whose first thought is always about how much will "it" cost. Unfortunately, here is where I asked myself—how much—instead of how this will change my life, the return on the investment, the potential to thrive, and most importantly, I did not ask myself "What do I want." See, as humans, we learn to focus on what could go wrong instead of all the great things that can and will happen if we just go for it.

Dan: Yes, you. You should just risk it all and go for it.

Carolina: No, Dan. It is not my time. But thank you for the trust.

Even though I said no back then, the fact that someone like him (I saw him and still see him as a great leader, mentor, and wonderful sponsor) told me I should go for it gave me hope or assurance that I could do anything. He knew what it would take. He had gone through this process and succeeded. And the fact that this accomplished, talented, smart white male executive of California thought this young (aka inexperienced) Latina woman could do it gave me hope.

The next couple of years, I proceeded to devour all things related to sustainability, leadership, business, empathy, innovation, teamwork, and everything in between.

Now, trust me. The path was not a straight line. I did read and learn, but a girl's gotta eat. Therefore, I had to, you know, work in between dreaming. I probably kept thinking about what was possible, but I knew I had to keep growing what I already had. And I was okay with that decision.

Fast-forward to December 2021, and I made up my mind again. I decided I was going back to school for a second master's degree. I had been through a transformative process the years before, and I was certain investing in my personal growth, meaningful relationships, and education were key to me thriving. Then, I was invited to visit Georgetown University–Edmund A. Walsh School of Foreign Service, to attend a class, more like a masterclass, by one of the talented professors. The day I set foot in that building, I knew that was the school for me. The class was phenomenal. Prof. Busch just shared so much info, and I probably understood only one-fourth of the terms used, but I knew this was the challenge I had yearned for ever since my conversation with Dan. It is only impossible until it's done. I applied, I wrote all the essays, asked for the recommendations (thanks, Bill & Rosario), prepared the videos, was part of their interview process, and got accepted. When I received my acceptance letter, I cried. The eleven-year-old girl inside of me could not believe my luck, perseverance, mindset, and power. Little Caro was SO proud.

Some of us dream of attending Georgetown, getting that promotion, building that empire, or building community. We all have dreams that can be scary to us. We have those voices inside and around us whispering why we can't do it or why we are not enough. But we need to remember that we have all the tools inside of us to overcome those fears and make those dreams a reality. Our brains and hearts are powerful, and whatever we dream, it is already there, ready for us. We just need to take the first step, and the second one, third, and so on. Take action and make it happen. And then, don't be discouraged by those swift changes. These are part of the process. Es más, enjoy the process. The good, the bad, and the ugly, because this is how we grow and evolve. At the end of the day, we all are #HumansInProgress building a life of purpose. And be ready to let go of some people in your life. We need to make room for other humans coming into our lives. We, as much as they learn from us, learn from them. It is part of the evolution.

And put yourself first always.

I know this is very un-Latino; we are taught to take care

of everyone else around us and not worry about ourselves. While it is a wonderful idea, it is unsustainable. We must take care of ourselves first, we must fill our cup (or gallon) first to then share our beauty, our love, our hearts with others. When we are in the plane, the flight attendants say "put your mask on first." We are more effective when we are ready to give out the best in us. And to do so, we need to take care of our hearts, minds, and bodies. We need to protect them as if we were protecting our parents or children, with everything we are.

And let's own our success. Be proud of your successes because these will come. It is your duty to celebrate and share these with everyone around you. By doing so, you will be showing others what is possible. Others will feel inspired by your drive and legacy, and they will then achieve their own dreams. Sin pena y con ganas.

I believe in you, now, just get out there and make it happen. I am rooting for you.

Our whole community is rooting for you!

REFLECT AND RISE

Step 1. Dare to dream big and believe in yourself. What do you want to accomplish and what are your steps to get there? Make a plan.

Step 2. Find mentors or allies that are going to

support you and hold you accountable. It is not about quantity, but quality.

Step 3. Take Action! Do weekly check-ins with your mentors/allies to review those goals you establish on step 1. Little progress is still progress. Persevere and you will get there. I believe in you!

BIOGRAPHY

Carolina Veira is an authentic leader, financial strategist, and Diversity and Inclusion champion, with a passion for the advancement and empowerment of women and communities of color.

Carolina is an award-winning Sustainability executive and entrepreneur with a successful trajectory in creating community initiatives and strategic partnerships. She believes in the power of building community by working together in financially sustainable initiatives that positively impact our global communities. At CareMax, Carolina leads the Sustainability strategy, where she makes ESG and purpose part of the DNA of CareMax, its mission, and its team members.

Carolina is the leader of The Hispanic Star Miami, steering the strategy, fundraising & development efforts of various initiatives benefiting the Hispanic Community and expanding organizational reach on a local and regional scale. Carolina also serves as a Board Director of Deliver the Dream, and she is part of the Healthcare and Sustainability Steering Committees at the South Florida Hispanic Chamber of Commerce.

Carolina is a contributing author to Hispanic Stars Rising: The New Face of Power, Today's Inspired Leader, Vol. III, and Today's Inspired Latina, Volume IX. Carolina believes our voices and our stories have unlimited power and need to be shared with the world, that is why she also hosts ¡HABLEMOS! Podcast: Conversations with talented humans who are leading with heart, and passion.

Carolina earned a double Bachelor of Science in Business and Accounting and an MBA from D'Youville University. She currently attends Georgetown University–Walsh School of Foreign Service, where she is working toward her master's in International Business and Policy. She is Ecuadorian American currently residing in Miami. She enjoys tennis, the Buffalo Bills, and speaks three languages.

> Carolina M. Veira
> Director of Partnerships, CSR, DEI
> Years in HR: 5
> info@carolinaveira.com
> Instagram/Twitter: @caroveira

UN DÍA A LA VEZ

YARED S. OLIVEROS

"To have courage for whatever comes in life—everything lies in that."
—St. Teresa of Avila

When I take a step back and reflect on what has shaped who I am, it truly goes back to my parents' courage leaving their home country, family, and all they had built. My dad left a career as an agriculturalist in Mexico where he was the first in his family to receive a master's degree. With the lack of resources left in Mexico, the only solution was to move to Los Angeles. I am sure my parents were terrified of all the uncertainty ahead. The only family we had there was able to accommodate us in their car garage. Although it wasn't physically a cozy place to live, our parents always made it feel like home through their love and presence.

Through their grit and tenacity to make ends meet, my parents took my brother and I for the ride. We helped Dad vacuum offices, took out the trash, and collected cans to recycle. We were not surrounded by role models in professional industries. My parents were just trying to survive and make sure we didn't get caught up in the gang mess that surrounded our neighborhood. But it was around that time in high school when my dad told me about his master's degree. I felt so proud of him! Although we didn't have what folks would consider the American Dream, we would have never known anything was missing from our lives. As I have grown into my own person, I owe a lot of who I am to my parents.

Our parents worked relentlessly to put us in private Catholic schools. Dad was working two jobs and still somehow managed to do service hours to help with financial aid obligations. My mother also worked just as hard to make sure we had everything the love of a mom can provide. I went to an all-girls Catholic high school, and being there played a big role in building my self-confidence as a woman, leader, and as an advocate for others.

DIOS SIEMPRE PROVEE

Initially, filling out financial aid and scholarship applications to go to college was exciting. But when I realized the amount received wasn't enough to attend a four year university, it was truly alarming and discouraging. My parents didn't think twice about taking out loans on my behalf and still encouraged me to attend. They would say, *"Dios siempre provee,"* and He truly has. I didn't know what I wanted to major in, but I was inspired by an amazing English professor who embodied so much of his love for people, the culture, and literature in his teachings. I decided to pursue an English major with a minor in Communications. It was a challenging four years as a commuter student. I worked part-time as a waitress, took a full load of classes, volunteered at my church, and somehow squeezed in non-paid internships at Telemundo, MTV, and Nickelodeon.

My parents and brother were still rooting for me along the way. They didn't always understand what I was doing, but the support was always there. All of these experiences have taught me to be strong and courageous on so many levels. Now, I try not to get discouraged, which happened a lot in the past. I always knew I was good at connecting with people and making them feel loved and special. This was my purpose, but how could I make a career out of it?

I have had so many wonderful mentors who have inspired and motivated me in various ways. While pursuing my master's degree, I met an inspiring woman who took me under her wing. To this day, she still guides me through tough career and life decisions. Her rawness and empathy have really helped me think through how each decision I make sets me up for success. God truly puts the right people in your life for a certain amount of time (some short periods, some longer periods) because He knows what is right for you. I remember when I was going to my interview at my first big girl career job at Nestlé in Glendale, California. I stood outside the twenty-one-story building and couldn't believe I was even being considered for an interview. I started to doubt whether I belonged there. I pulled myself together, said a prayer asking the Holy Spirit to guide me, and I leaned in. I got the job offer and, as you can imagine, I was full of sheer joy! In every role that I would apply for, from event planner, to college recruiter, to an HR generalist role and Diversity business partner role, it was always the same self-doubt. Nevertheless, my mentor, along with my family, were guiding me and praying on the sidelines. I wanted to make them all proud.

There have been times in my career where I felt so frustrated, embarrassed, ashamed, and alone. But I never let that stop me from being courageous. Remember that story in the Bible where Moses was in the desert for forty days and forty nights?! Yep, that's exactly how I felt. Sometimes even more now as a wife and a mother. Practicing the virtue of patience and humility has always been a challenge for me. I think God decided that by giving me two boys, they would help me to overcome it—He knows I am still trying! Needless to say, all of these experiences gave me the opportunity to work on virtues in different ways that led me to a career in HR. Practicing and living these virtues: generosity, diligence, patience, kindness, and humility is not easy. Nevertheless, this is what makes me work with an intentional heart to help feed people's desire to prosper, to know more, and to be better. Working in the space of Diversity, Equity and Inclusion, is not easy. The entire topic, role, definition, purpose, and framework is difficult to navigate. One is dealing with so many different views and inequities that it can be challenging to please everyone. However, I have learned being in this space that one needs to listen and be respectful regardless of my own views or general opinions. Being empathetic and understanding, following through, and having a true caring and loving spirit is part of how I have been able to approach it all.

BECAUSE WE CAN

Before I was married to my amazing husband and knee-deep in motherhood, I was a "free" bird just living my life without any worry in the world. I was exploring and traveling to many countries, embracing different cultures, and cultivating amazing relationships. I found myself in corners of the world where there was not just physical hunger but also a hunger to strive for more. It would tug at my heart, leaving me wondering what I could do and how I could help, especially in my own community.

In 2016, I had this strong calling that kept nudging me to put an event together for women in the city I grew up in. I leveraged my network and hosted my first "Because We Can" (BWC) event at my old high school, St. Mary's Academy. I secured four amazing diverse female panelists from different career fields and we had seventy-five women from all backgrounds attend this inspiring event. This platform allowed us to share our life and professional experiences with others. The best part of it all was getting feedback how this event impacted so many to make a positive change, and it validated how, together, we can make a difference.

This event set the stage for what would become one of my passion projects in Inglewood and now in my community in Northern California. The mission of BWC is to provide attendees with information and resources that will enable them to network, operate more effectively and efficiently in their current work environments, provide them with new career opportunities, or inspire them to start a new business. We do this by bringing a diverse group of individuals from various industries and backgrounds to share their stories and provide information that will help attendees identify their passion and create a plan for success. Currently, this project allows me to showcase my consultative skills by focusing on bridging the gaps with a different lens from the various experiences I have under my belt. My hope is to see Because We Can events hosted in multiple cities across the country in order to inspire countless women to boldly step into their dreams.

MAKE IT HAPPEN

In 2018, I had the opportunity to work for one of the most groundbreaking companies, Tesla! What?! Yes, folks, now that was intimidation at a whole other level. I remember walking the office floors the day of my interview and couldn't believe all the smart people that I could potentially be working alongside. I had not even started my interview and once again that impostor syndrome set in real quick. The question was, do I fit here? Of course I do! I made sure that I was going to be part of this amazing team. Working at Tesla has taught me to continue to be resilient, innovative, creative, and to not give up. I am still learning, still looking for ways to challenge myself, and keeping God in the center of it all.

In my current role as Diversity, Equity and Inclusion Business Partner and global employee resource group leader for our Latino community, one of my greatest accomplishments was taking a seemingly inactive ERG chapter in California to scaling and globally expanding our leadership and membership with over 1,000 members.

It has been a relentless team effort! Our focus is to drive employee retention by providing tools and resources that will help our Latino community close the wealth gap by being promoted into leadership roles. This role has allowed me to be a voice for the voiceless, influence our recruiting and sourcing efforts, as well as provide resources for our hiring managers in HR to help drive diversity in hiring, internal mobility, and employee referrals.

IBM, Institute for Business Value, recently surveyed Hispanics in the US to find out how professional advancement opportunities have played a crucial role in helping Latinos reach executive career success. For some context, the research shows that Latinos represent 18.5 percent of the population in this country but just 4 percent are in leadership roles. Diving more into this space, our young Latino junior managers stated that only 30 percent have access to mentorship programs or on-the-job training, 20 percent say they are empowered to overcome their professional challenges, and 67 percent say they have to work harder to succeed because of their identity. So how do I help influence and minimize the gap around overcoming professional challenges? I realized that what I am currently doing through the BWC events, through my influence within DEI, and my leadership with our employee resource group are ways to ignite change and contribute to my community.

All it takes is inspiring action and partnering together. Because together We Can.

REFLECT AND RISE

- What is your purpose? What are you good at?
- What excites you about the work that you are doing?
- How are you going to help other people with your talent(s) and give back to your community?

BIOGRAPHY

Yared Oliveros is a Senior Diversity & Inclusion Recruiting Business Partner at Tesla. Prior to joining this exciting role, she has served as a University Recruiter and is always leading with diversity initiatives in mind in order to recruit the best and the brightest talent for each team she supports, and it continues to be one of the most rewarding aspects of her role. She is currently Global President of the Latinos at Tesla employee resource group, and an active leader in her community where she puts together a yearly networking and inspirational event for local and nearby residents in her community, called Because We Can! Prior to joining Tesla, she began her career at Nestlé USA with diverse experiences under her belt such as program management, college recruiter, and an HR Business Partner, focusing on supporting the sales teams across the country. Yared is a graduate of Mount St. Mary's University, having received a bachelor's degree in English and a master's degree in Organizational Management from the University of Phoenix.

Yared S. Oliveros
Senior Diversity Equity and Inclusion Business Partner
Years in HR: 9
yaredsoliveros@gmail.com
LinkedIn.com/yaredoliveros
Instagram: @OneBecausewecan

BUILDING RESILIENCE THROUGH LIFE'S SEASONS

ARLENE RODRÍGUEZ

"We CAN do it all, just not all at once."

Fifteen years ago, I lay wide awake in bed wondering if I had made the right decision. I kept thinking, *Am I ready? Do I know enough? Am I good enough?* A few days earlier, my boss and dear mentor pulled me aside and encouraged me to take a rotational opportunity into human resources. She saw potential in me. In my young career at the time, I had just started settling into my first leadership role after a few trials and errors. I didn't know where this journey would take me, yet I was curious about HR and knew I had a passion for helping others. With all the nerves and excitement that come with facing change head on, I accepted this new challenge. Reflecting back, I realize how grateful I am for believing in myself and taking that next step in a journey built on evolving through life's ups and downs.

UNCHARTED WATERS

Those that know me well know that my family means everything to me. Like many, my parents migrated from Mexico and dreamed of starting a family with better life opportunities. They believed that investing time with loved ones was their purpose, and they humbly worked hard to provide a strong foundation for my younger sister and me. At a young age, I took pride in our rich Mexican culture, and it was in this environment that I knew I belonged. Everything I am and everything I have accomplished is because of them.

Life has a way of instantly changing. My pivotal moment came when I turned six and stepped forward into first grade. As I walked in toward my classroom, I quickly understood why my parents had mentioned it would be challenging at first. Up to that point, I had only spoken Spanish. Everyone and everything seemed foreign around me. I remember panicking and feeling a punch to my stomach as I held back the fear that began to consume me. I looked around, and even though I was fair skinned with blue eyes, I knew I was different and out of place. As a first-generation Mexican American, I grew up in a Spanish-speaking household and had not been exposed to the English language or the American culture before. I was used to seeing my extended family laughing and hugging as they came together, which was not the vibe I was getting from the other kids. This emotional day will forever be ingrained in my memory.

At the time, my school did not provide ESL resources, and with every fiber in me, I had to find the strength to preserve. Little did I know, speaking both languages would eventually enable me to become a young translator for my family. For years, I felt as if I was living in between two worlds, two cultures, two realities. Yet now, I see this bilingual skill as my superpower, one that allows me to extend a helping hand when needed and leverage my voice to advocate for others.

TRANSFORMING

My next big hurdle was navigating the unknown territory of continuing my education after high school. I lost focus in my studies in my senior year and I lacked awareness of career guidance and any resources available. After not being accepted to a university right away, I made the decision to alter my plans and spend the next few years at a community college to refocus on my grades. I was later officially accepted to UIC! That sense of accomplishment felt so good! Overcoming these challenges and adapting to different seasons of life at such a young age taught me how the process of building resilience is not straightforward. It ebbs and flows.

After graduation, my first gig was with a well-known general merchandise retailer, and I stepped in to lead a group of over fifty team members focused on guest experience. With great hustle, I built a healthy comradery within my team to accomplish our goals competitively. This task was far from easy and truly challenged me to grow as a leader. I had gone through extensive leadership training and tried to do everything perfectly, yet many of the methods I leveraged did not feel authentic to me. I would follow drafted scripts to coach coworkers, which led to awkward and strained work relationships. It felt as if my conversations lacked empathy, and while I was direct on what needed to be achieved, I did not gain the initial connection desired. I received sprinkles of feedback that indicated I was "too polished, too spicy, and lacked authenticity." With my head held high, I faked the impact these words had on me. I knew I was different and started to realize I was dealing with cultural conflicts. I thrived in an environment where goals were greater than reaching targets and deadlines. It was about bringing people together and celebrating each other through highs and lows. As in the past, I made the decision to change my approach and share my vulnerabilities with others. I paused and started to enable open lines of communication and build a team where people felt valued and seen.

While the results may have taken a bit longer to achieve, I knew we were creating a more unified, sustainable plan for the future. This was a pivotal moment for me and one that eventually opened the door to a rotation into human resources.

NEW DISCOVERIES

Early in my HR career, I was fortunate to work with so many people from different walks of life. I listened to their unique stories and diverse perspectives on how to solve challenges. This kept me grounded, and I longed to make a difference alongside them. This coworker population I supported reminded me of my own parents' aspirations and difficulties. I began advocating for them, using my superpower by translating their needs and leveraging my own voice to support more equitable and inclusive solutions. This opportunity felt so familiar given my own personal responsibilities I had early in life.

After a few years, my husband and I excitedly welcomed our first child, Alexandra. I had dreamed of being a mom and nurturing a family of my own for so long. In the first months, every moment with her fulfilled me and seemed surreal. At the same time, the thought of returning to work as I neared the end of my maternity leave consumed me. I was afraid to miss the little moments, and I knew it would be challenging to continue as an HR

Manager in retail with ten-hour shifts rotating at various times of day. One memory that vividly stands out for me is working an overnight shift while my daughter spiked a fever at home. It was heartbreaking and filled me with anxiety, as I now desired a different balance at this stage of my life. I turned to my family and vulnerably shared my struggles. I was burned out and couldn't do it any longer. Not only did I want to explore a different industry for greater flexibility, but I also considered taking a step back with my HR responsibilities. It was a hard decision to come to, as I was very career driven, but I knew I had the immense support of my husband and parents to follow the whispers of my heart. I saw this temporary adjustment as one that still took me to my destination but provided the opportunity to switch lanes where I could enjoy the moment even though it may take a few extra stops to get there.

I took a leap of faith and joined a Fortune 500 company in a corporate environment. I made the difficult decision to transition to a HR generalist position for greater balance. It was important for me to still grow professionally while being present at home with my growing family. I wanted to create my own path, one where I didn't have to stop enjoying what I did and still thrive by enhancing my HR skills. As my kids grew and became a bit more independent, I started to switch gears again and refocused my time and energy back in HR. I shared my aspirations with others and embraced opportunities that allowed me to continue rising to the top as an HR professional. I am a firm believer that we can do it all, just not all at once.

EVOLVING AS LEADER

Every now and then my kids ask, "Mom, what do you do at work?" I have found a simple answer along the lines of "I partner with others to make things happen" typically scratches the itch for them and provides a flavor of why I continue to enjoy the HR field. I find my work to be both rewarding and challenging. It has been a journey, since that first day of first grade, to find my authentic voice. I can now bring my quiet strength and unique experiences to the table and make a strong impact. It wasn't easy getting to this point, and I continue to learn as I evolve. I now know the value of true resilience, and it is my motivation in all aspects of my life.

REFLECT AND RISE

Below is some advice that I would offer to my younger self. These quick pointers have been my north star during challenging times and continue to ground me through my professional journey.

- **Believe in yourself:** Look inward and learn to advocate for yourself. Many of us have a tendency of putting ourselves last. Trust in your abilities and the value you bring. Chances are you already have a toolbox of skills and resources that have helped you overcome life experiences. Instead of doubting yourself, ask yourself, "Why not me?"

- **Have a growth mindset:** Take on new opportunities (i.e., projects, stretch assignments, rotations) and be curious. Growth is uncomfortable. You may not know all the answers, but trust that you will find a way through it.

- **Be resilient:** Ask for candid feedback from colleagues and be open (i.e., boss, direct reports, peers, internal clients). This can be done through a 1:1 discussion or a simple survey. Learn to use constructive feedback to your advantage. Bounce back quickly and don't let it distract you.

BIOGRAPHY

Arlene Rodríguez is a first-generation Mexican American born and raised in Chicago. Arlene is an HR leader that brings a balance of achieving business results and connecting with others at a human level. With her strong and humbling upbringing, she strives to continue to evolve as an authentic leader and inspire others to reach their full potential.

She is a graduate of the University of Illinois at Chicago. She holds a bachelor's degree in both Management and Marketing and has fifteen years of progressive experience in HR. In 2007, she started her HR career at Target overseeing talent initiatives with a concentration on recruitment, benefit enrollment, talent and performance management, employment relations, corporate policies, and succession planning. She currently works at CDW Corporation as a Senior Manager, HR Business Partner, where she has been instrumental in developing and driving talent strategies in areas of performance, development, engagement, and culture to enable and drive accelerated results. She is an active member of several BRGs, inclusive of HOLA (Hispanic Organization for Leadership and Achievement) and WON (Women's Opportunity Network), where she is purposeful in finding ways to evolve as a Latinx leader and give back to her community.

She is the mother of three beautiful children (Alexandra, Daniela, and Erik) and wife to her amazing husband, Erik. Her family is truly her pride and joy. Outside of work, Arlene enjoys traveling, coaching her kids through sport activities, and exploring the outdoors.

Arlene Rodríguez
Senior Manager, HR Business Partner
Years in HR: 15
Rodriguez.arlene31@gmail.com
Linkedin.com/in/rodriguez-arlene

RESOURCES:

As you begin looking for support and resources for yourself or your company, I invite you to consider participating and investing in these phenomenal organizations that continue to support our community in different ways:

- Association of Latino Professionals For America (ALPFA)
- Chicago United
- Congressional Hispanic Caucus Institute (CHCI)
- Diversity Best Practices
- DiversityInc
- DiversityMBA Magazine
- FairyGodBoss
- Fig Factor Foundation
- Hispanic Alliance for Career Enhancement (HACE)
- Hispanic Association of Colleges and Universities (HACU)
- Hispanic Association on Corporate Responsibility (HACR)
- Hispanic Executive
- Hispanic Inspiring Student's Performance and Achievement (HISPA)

- Hispanic Star
- HRHotseat
- Human Resource Certification Institute (HRCI)
- Human Rights Campaign (HRC)
- HR in Jeans
- LatinaPro
- Latinas in Architecture
- Latinas in Real Estate
- Latinas In Tech
- Latinas in Wellness
- Latinas Rising Up In HR Network - this is us :)
- Latino Corporate Directors Association (LCDA)
- Latino Leaders Magazine
- L'attitude
- League of United Latin American Citizens (LULAC)
- #LovePurse
- National Association of Women Business Owners (AWBO)
- National Hispanic Corporate Council (NHCC)
- Network of Executive Women (NEW)
- Poderista
- Prospanica (Association of Hispanic MBAs & Business Professionals)

RESOURCES

- Society of Hispanic Professionals in Engineering (SHPE)
- Society of Human Resource Management (SHRM)
- Techqueria | Latinx in Tech
- The Autism Hero Project
- The Latinista
- The Latino Hive
- The Mom Project
- UnidosUS
- United Latinas
- United States Hispanic Chamber of Commerce
- We All Grow Latina
- We Are All Human
- Working Mother Media

ABOUT THE AUTHOR

About the Author

Priscilla Guasso is dedicated to unlocking the keys to connections and communities.

She is a talented, energetic, and driven woman who instinctively sees the potential of others and connects them to their mission by embracing their curiosities to help reveal the purposeful leader they have inside.

A skilled human resources leader, Priscilla has focused on all areas of the employee life cycle: talent acquisition, mobility, talent development, succession planning, performance management, employee relations, global diversity, equity and inclusion, and overall company culture.

With global HR experience since 2006 in the US, Latin America, the Caribbean, the UK, and Canada, Priscilla has spent a great deal of time in the hospitality and healthcare industries. Today, she's a leader in the talent management, development, and diversity team within the technology industry.

Through her business, Manifesting Leadership Group, LLC, Priscilla coaches and trains leaders in corporate, start-ups, nonprofit, and government agencies, giving them opportunities to invest in themselves to effectively grow their leadership skills.

As an Amazon best-selling author and founder of Latinas Rising Up In HR®, she continues to give back by creating a community of Latinas in HR and their allies, sharing their keys of knowledge and success, and opening doors to unlimited possibilities.

Priscilla holds a Bachelor of Science degree in business administration with a concentration in marketing from the University of Illinois, Urbana–Champaign. She is a popular and in-demand speaker known for her vulnerability and touching on topics in personal development, DEI, allyship, combating your inner critic, and embracing failure.

In 2021, she became a contributing author to Volume 9 of Today's Inspired Latina™, was a speaker for the 2021 LATINATalks Global Tour, and has served as a proud board member of the Fig Factor Foundation.

During the 2020 pandemic, Negocios Now recognized Priscilla as a Latino 40 Under 40. She is also an annual inspiration agent for Young Latina Day and a proud member of HRHotseat, Hispanic Star Miami, Society of Human Resources Management (SHRM), and The Latinista. She is also a past board member of the National Hispanic Corporate Council (NHCC), Mujeres de HACE Chicago, and the Latino/Latina Alumni Association for the University of Illinois.

Based in Miami and Chicago, Priscilla enjoys traveling to new cities with her husband, Jorge, spending time with close family, and soaking up the sun in warmer climates.

Follow me at www.linkedin.com/in/priscillaguasso
Connect on IG @priscillaguass @latinasinhr
Email: Info@LatinasRisingUpInHR.com
www.PriscillaGuasso.com
www.LatinasRisingUpInHR.com